# Yorkshire by Rail

## A guide to the routes, scenery and towns

# FOREWORD

**by James Towler**
**Chairman, Transport Users' Consultative Committee (TUCC) for Yorkshire 1979–1985, for North East England, 1985–1987**

I am particularly pleased to have been asked to contribute an introduction to this engrossing book, which is one of a series being published under the auspices of the Railway Development Society. It is, I believe, a splendid example of how the interest and enthusiasm of a fairly small number of railway *aficionados* can be deployed to capture the imagination of a far wider public.

Over the years, I have had many useful contacts with the RDS and its associated user groups. Those that come most vividly to mind relate to the many British Rail closure proposals within Yorkshire and the subsequent hearings at which I have presided. It is on these occasions that the RDS and its members come into their own. The evidence they present to support the case for the retention of a station or line is invariably well documented and researched, often more so than the case for closure.

It is, perhaps, ironic that it has been the threat of line closures which has often provided the motivation that has resulted in the formation of many of the local user groups in Yorkshire. While one closure proposal has become a national *cause célèbre*, there can be few who have not heard of Settle–Carlisle, others less known, like the intriguingly labelled Goose Hill–Wath Road or the faintly erotic-sounding Five Curves, have not been neglected by the RDS.

Nor should opposition to railway closures be considered a negative or purely emotive attitude. Providing there is a good case to retain a station or line, a well-organised campaign–in which the local user group or groups often play a major role–can achieve the desired result. It should not be forgotten that the 'battle' for the 'Bridge over the River Ouse' (Goole–Gilberdyke) was actually won before it went to a public hearing.

However, the activities of the RDS are by no means confined to fighting railway closures. In many instances local user groups have established a rapport with British Rail and the local authorities which has led to improved marketing and the provision of better services on a specific line. I know one case where British Rail adopted a timetable submitted by a user group as it was better than its own!

Indeed enlightened railway managers are increasingly looking to the RDS and local user groups as allies in their efforts to provide the best possible rail service within the financial and other constraints they operate. As the statutory rail-users' watch-dog, the TUCC welcome this trend. For while some of British Rail's more bizarre decisions invite adverse criticism, at the end of the day all of us who use the railway want to see it succeed.

*Leeds, October 1986*

# Dedication

The RDS Yorkshire Branch wish to dedicate this volume to the memory of
**Eric Treacy**
(1907–1978)
Right Reverend Bishop of Wakefield, 1968-76
Adoptive Yorkshireman, lifelong rail enthusiast,
and patron of rail travellers everywhere

*Front cover: Duchess of Hamilton* hauls a special–'Limited Edition'– over Knaresborough Viaduct in 1980. *(Photo: George Wood)*
*Back cover:* The historic city of York *(Photo E. A. Woodall)*
*Title page:* A Trans-Pennine train approaches Standedge Tunnel, Marsden, with the canal, picnic spot and beyond, the Countryside Centre *(Photo: David Thurlow)*

# CONTENTS

# INTRODUCTION

**by the Editors, Philip Ralph and Mike Crowhurst**

What is Yorkshire? A county, a region, or a province? A way or life—or a state of mind? The editors, not being born or bred Yorkshiremen, are perhaps less qualified than most to answer such philosophical questions, but we have come to appreciate many of the attractions of Yorkshire that are often overlooked by the outsider. Ironically the remoter upland areas such as the Dales, the North York Moors, and the coast are probably better known outside Yorkshire than are the towns and cities, which are often dismissed as industrial wildernesses. Those who make this assumption are guilty of a grave error and miss much of interest. Even in 'urban' Yorkshire, the cities and towns are still identifiably separate places, with surprising amounts of countryside remaining between them. These areas, dotted with small towns, villages, farms, textile mills, and smallholdings stretching right up into the Pennines, are just as rewarding to the rambler or cyclist as the remoter country of North and East Yorkshire. What is more, they are still blessed with remarkably good public transport—both rail and bus.

The cities themselves are rich in museums, civic architecture, and examples of our cultural and industrial heritage, and not least, of our transport heritage. Yorkshire boasts two transport museums, several 'preserved' railways, and a still-functioning canal network, as well as much to interest the bus, trolleybus, or tram enthusiast. Metropolitan Yorkshire, in short, is an area of ever-changing contrasts. This is not to say that we have neglected the wilder parts of Yorkshire, or at least not those still accessible by rail, for in the coast and Dales of Yorkshire we have some of the most magnificent scenery in England still easily reached by rail. We have sought to maintain a balance between the urban and rural facets of Yorkshire.

This volume is one of a series produced by branches of the Railway Development Society in various parts of the country, and readers familiar with earlier volumes in this series will know that we do not seek to provide a comprehensive tourist guide (these can be obtained from the appropriate Tourist Information Offices, whose addresses are to be found at the end of this volume), nor a detailed railway history or enthusiasts' guide—there are plenty of those on the market already! Nor do we wish to compete with the British Rail Timetable, although some general information of use to the passenger is included.

What we do aim to do is to provide an introductory guide for the rail-oriented visitor, to describe what can be seen from the train, suggest places of interest that can be easily reached by rail, and whet the appetite for a return visit. Each chapter is written by local people who use the line regularly (and in some cases have been closely involved in fights to save and develop their line) and many of the illustrations have been provided by the authors and other members of the line users' groups.

The question 'What is Yorkshire?' has been further complicated since 1974 by bureaucratic tinkering with boundaries, so that neither current administrative boundaries, historic boundaries, nor (least of all!) BR regional boundaries exactly define the area covered by this book. We have taken a practical approach, and sought to fit sensibly with the coverage of our neighbouring branches in their sister volumes. Thus we have included North Humberside (which is Yorkshire by any sensible definition), but not South Humberside, which is covered in *Lincolnshire by Rail.* Similarly the Eskdale and North York Moors lines in the Whitby area, while undeniably Yorkshire, are somewhat isolated from the rest of the Yorkshire rail network and in any event are admirably described in *North-East by Rail,* so are not covered in this volume.

In some cases overlap is inevitable: neither this volume nor *Lancashire and Cumbria by Rail* would be complete without a chapter on the Settle–Carlisle line. In most cases the territory described begins or ends at a major railway centre (Manchester, Sheffield, Doncaster, Darlington), but some routes are necessarily split between adjoining volumes. The Sheffield–Retford route, together with the Hope Valley line, will be found in *Five Shires by Rail*, covering the North and East Midlands. The map on the centre pages shows the lines covered in relation to adjoining lines. We have included all lines within this area upon which regular passenger services are run, but not those lines on which the only scheduled passenger services are a handful of seasonal trains (mostly at dead of night or crack of dawn) such as Halifax–Huddersfield and the Normanton–Rotherham section of the Midland route between Leeds and Sheffield, especially since both these routes have now been approved for closure. That is not to say that the reader will never find himself travelling (unexpectedly) over these lines, as they are still in frequent use for diversions.

One final point, regarding *buses*. Regular bus-users will not need reminding that the fabled Chinese curse 'May you live in interesting times' is coming to pass with a vengeance on the buses, as Nicholas Ridley's Transport Act comes into force. South Yorkshire fares have already been massively increased in April 1986. At the time of writing in October 1986 (the run-up to D-day), it looks as if the immediate effects in fortunate areas may be confined to a blossoming of unfamiliar liveries and the loss of certain handy tickets like the Dales Wayfarer or South Yorkshire's Out & About ticket. But from January 1987 almost anything can happen at about six weeks' notice, and it is generally agreed that evening, Sunday, and rural services will be most at risk, with much depending on budgets determined by Government. In these circumstances it is pointless including detailed bus information which may be hopelessly inaccurate by the time the book appears on sale in 1987. We have, therefore, included only general information on bus services, and strongly advise would-be users to contact the relevant transport authority for details before travelling. The addresses are given at the end of this volume. Heaven forbid that similar legislation should ever be inflicted on the railways!

Looking towards Bolton Abbey from the Cow and Calf rocks, Ilkley Moor (*Photo: Yorkshire and Humberside Tourist Board*)

# 1

# EAST COAST MAIN LINE – GATEWAY TO YORKSHIRE

## DONCASTER–YORK–DARLINGTON

**by Trevor Garrod**

Many visitors reach Yorkshire by the East Coast main line – the InterCity route from London King's Cross to Edinburgh which slices its way across the county via Doncaster, York, and Darlington. High Speed Trains travelling at up to 125 mph can cover the 156 miles from London to Doncaster in as little as ninety-eight minutes. Some of them continue northwards up the main line to York and beyond; others branch off north-westwards towards Wakefield and Leeds.

Doncaster, the first town in Yorkshire, is heralded by pit-heads and trains of coal-hoppers which appear out of the countryside to the west; and the main line curves gently past the famous racecourse to the east. Sandwiched between the junctions on the approach to Doncaster, protected by the surrounding lines, is Potteric Carr Nature Reserve, administered by the Yorkshire Wildlife Trust. Soon we are entering the town's busy station, junction for Sheffield, Cleethorpes, Hull, Selby, and Leeds. To the left are the locomotive works established soon after the Great Northern Railway reached Doncaster in 1851. To the right is the town's shopping centre and, beyond that, the market area, dominated by a parish church of cathedral-like proportions.

Our northbound train may now take the main line proper, across the flat farmland of the Vale of York, or the route to Leeds through contrasting scenery of hills peppered with mining villages. To the main line first: we speed past Bentley Colliery to the west and out across lush open fields and meadows studded from time to time with clusters of cooling towers. These belong to a series of power-stations built in the 1960s and 1970s: Thorpe Marsh to the east, then Eggborough to the west and, shortly after, Drax a few miles away to the east.

Hundreds of feet below us, though you probably would not realise it, are the seams of Selby coalfield, one of the newest and largest in the country, which recently started production. That is why, after crossing the meandering River Aire, High Speed Trains veer left at Temple Hirst Junction on to the newest main-line railway in Great Britain. This is the Selby diversion, opened in October 1983 to avoid subsidence caused by the new coal-workings. The line cuts its way with ease across fields and woodlands, spanned by concrete road bridges, and on it the High Speed Trains can reach their 125 mph maximum.

Looking to the north-east, we can see the tower of the medieval Selby Abbey; before 1983 our train would have given a much closer view of it, as it still served this small market town. Now Selby has to rely instead on a DMU shuttle to Doncaster and York plus the Leeds–Hull cross-country trains. The line carrying these trains passes over ours at Hambleton Junctions, after which we continue northward, soon crossing another slow winding river – the Wharfe – before joining the Sheffield–York line at

Colton Junction. We speed through Copmanthorpe village—suggested by some as a good site for a reopened station—and reach the outskirts of York. Chaloners Whin Junction is a junction no more—but a cutting to the east marks the now-abandoned course of the old main line north of Selby.

Almost all trains call at York's majestic station with its curving train shed and fifteen platforms, completed in 1877. It is an architectural monument in its own right and a fitting introduction for the many visitors to this great city—described in detail in Chapter 2.

As the train leaves York, look across at the National Railway Museum to the left. After negotiating the curves, the train gathers speed past Skelton Junction, under the shadow of the British Sugar Corporation factory, and then heads north-westwards over mile upon mile of straight, flat, quadruple track across the northern part of the Vale of York. There are no large towns here and all but two of the stations on the 44-mile run from York to Darlington had closed by 1960. Top expresses speed through the two remaining stations, Thirsk and Northallerton, but semi-fast trains call there, giving these two market towns and their wide catchment area a very reasonable service.

As we speed across the Vale, note the sign near Tollerton indicating that we are now half-way from London to Edinburgh and, on the right side of the line, the unusual Sidings Restaurant composed of restored railway coaches. Further to the north-east, the Howardian Hills and the North York Moors are looming up, with a white horse cut into one prominent hillside.

Just over 22 miles from York, Thirsk Station with its two island platforms, recently improved with a District Council grant, is about a mile from the town centre, past the well-known racecourse. The town has a Gothic parish church and a museum. Both Thirsk and Northallerton are useful railheads for cycling trips, with many miles of

A northbound High Speed Train pulls away from York with the Minster in the background *(Photo: British Rail)*

flat pleasant country and quiet roads around them and the North York Moors close at hand.

Northallerton is 7¾ miles on from Thirsk and slightly larger. The town grew up as a market and staging post on the main road, and later became important for its railway workshops, now closed. It is also the administrative centre of North Yorkshire and County Hall can be seen, amid trees, just to the east of the station.

The quadruple main line now becomes double track, and an avoiding line allows freight trains bound for Teesside to pass to the west of Northallerton Station before rumbling under the main line and off towards Eaglescliffe. The station itself, on an embankment, is denuded of some of its earlier buildings, though some local-authority-financed improvements have now been made, and it gives good views across the town towards the ornate 14th century church tower.

As the train gathers speed for the next stage north, note a single track trailing in from the west–the Wensleydale freight line to Leyburn and Redmire. Its main traffic is limestone from Redmire Quarry for British Steel; but since 1978 it has also been used for more than a dozen excursion trains bringing visitors to the dale and providing days out for local people. There are currently three or four buses a day from Northallerton to Leyburn, some of which connect with trains; and at Leyburn you can catch buses to go farther up the dale.

Soon the Moors are receding to the east, but the distant Pennines take shape on the north-west horizon. We shoot across the winding River Tees in its tree-lined gorge, out of Yorkshire and into County Durham. Soon we are drawing into the main-line station at Darlington, a town rich in railway history and an ideal gateway for exploring the North East–armed with our companion volume, *North East by Rail.*

## DONCASTER–WAKEFIELD–LEEDS

**by Trevor Garrod and Mike Crowhurst**

The 30-mile route from Doncaster to Leeds, like the main line, is due to see electric trains in 1989. At present it has High Speed Trains and a local railcar service. The area through which it passes contrasts remarkably with the flat, rich, rural Vale of York.

The Leeds line threads its way around the Yorkshire coalfield and is rarely out of sight of red-brick towns, estates, and pit villages. It leaves the main line at Marshgate Junction, just outside Doncaster Station, heads north-west to Adwick Junction where it is joined by the freight line from Thorpe Marsh power-station, then heads into the rolling hills to the west. Local trains call at South Elmsall, the first station in West Yorkshire and the only small station left open on this route when all the others were closed in the 1960s.

A mile or so beyond South Elmsall, the Sheffield (Swinton & Knottingley) line passes over the main line, and a curve coming in immediately afterwards on the left brings Sheffield–Leeds InterCity trains on to the main line; these trains have used this route for the last few years in place of the traditional Midland route via Normanton. The junction at South Kirkby is in the midst of a landscape of pits and spoil-heaps that forms the South Kirkby Colliery complex (still rail-served).

The next few miles take us past the mining townships of Hemsworth and Fitzwilliam. A two-platform unstaffed halt was opened at Fitzwilliam on 1 March 1982, the first such station to be opened by the now-disbanded West Yorkshire Metropolitan County Council. A little over a mile from Fitzwilliam, on the Wakefield–Doncaster main road, is Nostell Priory and Park, a National Trust property and home of Lord St Oswald. The house, which is open to the public at certain times during the summer months, dates from 1733 and is built on the site of a medieval priory. It is effectively hidden from the railway line by Nostell Colliery. Buses run on the road between Fitzwilliam and Nostell, or direct from Wakefield or Doncaster.

Soon the broad Calder Valley opens out ahead and the outskirts of Wakefield close in. The city skyline is dominated by the towers of the Cathedral, the Town Hall, and the County Hall. The line approaches the city on a long curving viaduct, the so-called 'Ninety-nine Arches', which carries it over the River Calder, the former Lancashire & Yorkshire main line and a number of roads. As we pass over that line, Wakefield Kirkgate Station is clearly visible to the east, and the short curve linking the two stations (and used by the shuttle service to Huddersfield) trails in on the right shortly before the end of the viaduct. On the opposite side, a glimpse of Sandal Castle ruins can be had to the south as the train crosses the river.

The train runs off the viaduct into Wakefield Westgate Station. this station was largely rebuilt in smart functional style in 1967 and is now firmly established as Wakefield's principal station. It was not always so, however – its rival at Kirkgate predates it by seventeen years, and was long the busier and more opulent of the two. Today Westgate Station, conveniently sited on the western edge of the city centre, is a popular InterCity railhead for businessmen who drive from many parts of West Yorkshire to join the London train here in preference to Leeds. The station (or rather a yard just north of it) is also a transhipment point for new cars, which can be seen stored on the right of the line below the County Hall.

# WAKEFIELD

**by Mike Crowhurst and Steve Wiltshire**

Wakefield has been an important centre of local government for many years. Incorporated as a Borough in 1848, it was chosen as the seat of the new County Council of the West Riding in 1888 due to its central position in the growing industrial area between the cities of Leeds and Sheffield. In that same year of 1888 it was created a Diocese and its parish church elevated to the status of cathedral. In 1974 the West Riding County Council was replaced by the short-lived West Yorkshire Metropolitan County Council, abolished in 1986, with the result that Wakefield now shares with London the distinction of having a redundant Victorian County Hall. The city still houses a number of county-wide bodies such as the Passenger Transport Executive and the County Police Headquarters. (It also has a prison – located right next to Westgate Station!) Being on the fringe of both mining and textile areas, Wakefield has a varied industrial and commercial life.

The visitor to Wakefield arriving at Westgate Station has a short walk up Westgate into the city centre. First impressions are not encouraging from this direction, but just after the first traffic lights the newly restored Theatre Royal and Opera House can be seen on the left. At the top of the hill, as the road winds round the Yorkshire Bank, a series of pedestrian streets fork off to the right; those in a hurry to reach Kirkgate Station should go that way. A little farther along, the road brings us to the Bull Ring, the central point of the city, with its somewhat incongruous statue of Queen Victoria, newly restored amid much civic controversy in 1985 to her position in the reorganised intersection, after a temporary sojourn in a park on the outskirts of the city. The bus station is to be found just beyond the Bull Ring in Union Street.

A right turn at the Bull Ring into the pedestrian area brings us to the Cathedral. Its spire, the city's most prominent landmark, is the tallest in Yorkshire, 247 feet high. The origin of the building is uncertain but it reached its present form in 1905 and there has been a church on the site for at least 900 years. Tucked away behind the Cathedral is its most recent addition, an attractive octagonal meeting-room, the Treacy Memorial Hall. This was completed in 1982 and commemorates the late Bishop

The Treacy Memorial Hall, Wakefield Cathedral *(Drawing: Peter Marshall, Courtesy Friends of Wakefield Cathedral)*

Eric Treacy, 'The Railway Bishop', to whom this book is dedicated.

Continuing past the Cathedral in the same direction brings us to the main entrance to The Ridings, Wakefield's award-winning indoor shopping centre, a three-level complex opened in 1983. The lower entrance leads into Kirkgate, which can also be reached by following the pedestrian street below the Cathedral if you prefer the open air. Those looking for Kirkgate Station turn right in Kirkgate, use the subway under the Chantry roundabout, and turn into a side road on the left at the traffic lights to find the station (¾ mile from Westgate). A little farther on, beyond the railway bridge, is the fourteenth-century Chantry Chapel, built on to the old road bridge over the River Calder, one of the city's smallest and most unusual buildings.

Back in the city centre, those with rather more time may care to turn north into Wood Street, which leaves the route to or from Westgate one block west of the Bull Ring. This is Wakefield's Civic Parade – after a few shops we have four nineteenth-century Municipal buildings in a row on the left: first the City Museum (1820), then the Town Hall (1880), the Court House (1810), and the County Hall (1898), while opposite is the Police Station and at the far end in rather different style, the modern buildings of the District College. Continuing past the college into Wentworth Street leads us shortly to St John's Square (just under ½ mile from the Bull Ring), an area of pleasant Georgian town houses set round a church in the centre of the square, now a Conservation Area. The street opposite the church, St John's North, is an extension of the same development, and leads us into Northgate, by which we can return to the Bull Ring, passing the Queen Elizabeth Grammar School on the far side.

Among places of interest reached from Wakefield, the most accessible is Sandal Castle (2 miles) which is reached by a short ride on any of the Barnsley Road buses (which pass Kirkgate Station), alighting at the Three Houses Inn, and following the signposts along Manygates Lane. The castle dates from the twelfth century and was the site of hostilities in the Wars of the Roses and in the Civil War. The site is always open, and the view over the city from the mound is worth the trip. Other places of interest accessible by bus from Wakefield include Bretton Country Park (home of the

Yorkshire Sculpture Park), the conserved village of Heath and its common and, as mentioned earlier, Nostell Priory.

## WAKEFIELD–LEEDS

After our exploration of Wakefield we must resume our journey to Leeds. As we leave Westgate Station a view opens out briefly to the left over some open land to Alverthorpe Church, prominent on a hilltop, and beside it the buildings of Silcoates Hall School. The line then cuts through the suburb of Wrenthorpe (which has also been considered for a new local station), before climbing again to higher land. A bleaker landscape takes over, punctuated by the remains of Lofthouse Colliery and then the overbridges of the M1 and M62. There are no local stations open on this section today, branches to Dewsbury, Rothwell, and Morley have long since gone, but the span of some of the older bridges over the main line still bear witness to the scale of railway operations at Ardsley marshalling yard in the past.

As we emerge from the short Ardsley Tunnel, the town of Morley can be seen perched starkly on the hill to the west, and the Leeds suburb of Middleton, although not visible, is even closer on the eastern side on another hill. Our train is descending again now as we wind our way among the arterial roads, factories, and tower blocks on the approach to Leeds. Followers of football will recognise Leeds United's Elland Road Ground on the right just before the line crosses the M621 motorway; there are plans to build a 'Hooligan Halt' here, to enable visiting supporters to detrain directly into the ground. Shortly after crossing the Gelderd Road the train will probably make a sharp turn to the right, crossing back over the Gelderd Road to take the viaduct approach to Leeds Station. This route passes over the Woodlesford line, with a fine view of the Holbeck locomotive yard, before joining the other lines for the final approach to the station. This section of line, originally connected to the LNWR's Huddersfield line, has been the usual approach route for London trains in recent years, but is due to be taken out of service as part of the electrification work. The approach will then be via the Wortley curve, which passes over the Huddersfield line before joining the Huddersfield and Bradford lines simultaneously. If your train goes this way, look out for the remains of the Wortley West curve on the left, which used to give a direct route to Bradford but was disconnected in 1985 on safety grounds at the behest of the Railway Inspectors, to the disgust of Bradford City Council and of local user groups who wanted to see it retained and used for electric services to Bradford. British Rail did not even consider it necessary to go through the statutory closure procedure.

As the train picks its way through the series of junctions on the western approach to the large modernised station, the thin white tower of the University can be seen on the hill to the north, above terraces of housing. No one would rank Leeds with Harrogate, York, or Scarborough as a tourist centre, yet it is very much the hub of the Yorkshire rail network, and is ideally placed for exploring the rest of Yorkshire by rail. Leeds is the limit of 'Industrial' Yorkshire; beyond the leafy suburbs to the north of the city (themselves broken by green wedges such as Roundhay Park, Meanwood, and the Aire Valley itself) stretch the rural delights of moors and dales, many of them easily reached by one of the seven or eight lines radiating from Leeds.

## INTRODUCTION TO LEEDS

**by Philip Ralph**

Like many northern industrial cities, Leeds grew up with the Industrial Revolution. Something of the long-established Leeds engineering industry, the close association with coal-mining, and the history and development of the important clothing and printing industries, can be seen by visiting the Leeds Industrial Museum at Armley Mills, off Canal Road. Take a Kirkstall Road bus from City Square outside the station, and alight at Canal Road by the viaduct on the Harrogate line. The Industrial Museum is open daily except Sunday mornings and Mondays. The same bus will take you to Kirkstall Abbey ruins, farther along Kirkstall Road, which are clearly visible from trains on the Airedale line and not far from Headingley Station on the Harrogate line (See Chapter 5).

Today's visitor arriving in Leeds by rail is immediately aware of the importance of business and commerce in the economy of Leeds, and its impact on the changing skyline of the city. The growth of both public and private service industries has reinforced the strategic importance of the city of over half a million population, at the hub of the Yorkshire Region. In the private sector, modern shopping complexes such as Bond Street and the Merrion Centre are prominent features, along with banking and insurance offices. The public sector is well represented, beginning on the Headrow with a typical imposing North of England Town Hall, behind which is to be found the graceful structure of the Civic Hall, seat of local administration since 1933. Between here and Headingley lie both the University and the Polytechnic, and on nearby Cookridge Street is the Roman Catholic Cathedral of St Anne.

There is a lively cultural atmosphere in Leeds. It boasts two regionally important theatres and the famous City Varieties Music Hall; it is the home of Opera North and plays host to prestigious musical concerts and festivals. The Art Gallery, near the Town Hall, and the open-air life-size public chess-boards, commemorate the work of the Yorkshire sculptor, the late Henry Moore, who had strong local connections. The Henry Moore Sculpture outside the Art Gallery will shortly have a companion (a 100-foot man), to be built on railway land in the Holbeck Triangle on the south-western approach to the station. Those with less highbrow tastes may prefer the attractions of Temple Newsam House and Grounds in the eastern suburbs, reached by No. 22 bus from City Square or the Corn Exchange or on foot from Crossgates Station (see the next chapter).

# THE MIDDLETON RAILWAY, HUNSLET, LEEDS

**by John Bushell**

No description of Yorkshire railways would be complete without mention of the oldest railway in the world and main attraction in Leeds for the transport enthusiast. This little line has a long history, having been authorised in 1758 by the first Railway Parliamentary Act. In 1811 the enterprising John Blenkinsop patented a rack-and-pinion steam locomotive, and Matthew Murray built the world's first commercially successful steam locomotive the following year. Remarkably, the railway has survived, and today you will find a regular week-end passenger service from Easter to September, connecting Hunslet Moor with Middleton Woods. A goods train runs 'as required' between British Rail's Balm Road and Robinson's & Birdsall's Yard. The collection of small steam and diesel locomotives is on display at week-ends throughout the year. Approximately 2 miles of track is used today, and the sound of a steam loco still resounds around Middleton after over 175 years. Any Dewsbury Road bus from the Corn Exchange will take you to Tunstall Road, from which the Moor Road Station is five minutes' walk. By car, the station adjoins Junction 45 on the M1, and is signposted at this exit (car park available). For futher information write : The Station, Moor Road, Hunslet, Leeds, or telephone Leeds 645424.

# 2

# YORKSHIRE'S OLDEST MAIN-LINE RAILWAY

## THE LEEDS & SELBY RAILWAY

**by John Bushell**

Although the Stockton & Darlington (1825) and Liverpool & Manchester (1830) predate this 1834 route, the first main line in Yorkshire was an innovative and forward-looking enterprise. We leave Leeds City (formerly 'New' Station of 1869) over a viaduct, passing the domed Corn Exchange (1868) and the White Cloth Hall (1775) on the left. The railway runs over the graves of Leeds Parish Churchyard on the right, the embankments being paved in tombstones. There are proposals under consideration for a station here to link with the nearby Central Bus Station. The present Victorian church boasts a Saxon Cross, evidence of a long history. Unusually it boasts a tradition of the choir singing a daily Evensong.

Marsh Lane Station closed on 13 September 1958. The original terminus was between the line and the present cement siding. Here began one of the wonders of the line, the first tunnel through which steam-hauled passenger trains ran. Attempts were made to lure passengers into the darkness by whitewashing the walls and using copper reflectors. In 1894 it was widened into a deep cutting. Beyond the east end of the cutting is Neville Hill (junction for Hunslet East Oil Depot) and the Eastern Region's maintenance depot for all InterCity 125 trains as well as the humble local diesel trains. Osmondthorpe housing estate was served by a halt between 1930 and 1960. It is currently on the list of possible new halts in West Yorkshire. As we speed eastwards over the Selby Road, note the bridge, built for four tracks, described in 1834 as an 'astonishing display of industry and art'.

The first station today is Crossgates, until 1964 junction for Wetherby and Harrogate. Temple Newsam House, 'The Hampton Court of the North' is set in 935 acres of parkland 1 mile south of the station. Dating back to Tudor and Jacobean times, it is now a treasure-house owned by Leeds City Council.

Garforth Station serves a growing commuter town. Until 1957 it was the junction for Kippax and Castleford. An additional station is due to open at East Garforth in May 1987. At one time, an independent company linked the Leeds & Selby Railway to Aberford, serving coal-mines and the village. Today the trackbed makes an interesting walk across Parington Park, through rolling wooded countryside to a coaching village now (fortunately) deserted by the Great North Road. The Norman church (unusually dedicated to the seventh century French missionary St Ricarius) is rich in wooded carvings. Nearby is Lotherton Hall Bird Park, and at its doorstep another Norman church.

Micklefield is the junction for York. The most notable feature of this nondescript colliery village is the 1834 station. The early goods warehouse, porters' room, and station-master's house are close to the fine underbridge. Goods were lifted by hoist to a rail-level storage area. The 43-foot-deep cutting that follows has several bridges, described by the French engineer Letillier (1833) as 'superior to any of their kind in England'.

South Milford has a semi-derelict 1834 station with original low platform, from which travellers of 150 years ago would have to clamber into the train!

The line rises now to cross the York & North Midland opened in 1840. Gascoigne Wood (or Milford Old Junction) was, in the nineteenth century, the changing-point for York travellers. The site of the busy marshalling yards have received a new lease of life from the development of the Selby coalfield. Although the work-force has access to the seams elsewhere, all coal is distributed by rail from this busy yard with its advantageous 'hub' position, in the Yorkshire rail network.

Hambleton Station closed to passengers in 1959. Today it is the the point where Yorkshire's oldest main line crosses its newest, the 1983 main line, built to avoid anticipated new coalfield subsidence near Selby.

Selby is today a railway backwater since losing the London–Edinburgh (1983), Cawood (1929), Goole (1964), and Market Weighton & Driffield (1965) services. In 1834, Selby was the 'port of Leeds'. Today sea-going vessels continue to serve the wharves and factories, while Cochrane's Shipyard builds trawlers, tugs, and coastal passenger vessels. Take a look at the extensive remains of the 1834 station, and the rotting quay to the south of the present building. Booking of tickets was in the Station-Master's House. Passengers and goods shared the 240-foot-long timber shed. As the station only saw six years of passenger use, it is a remarkable survival. Before 1840, rail passengers made the 43-mile river journey to Hull on the notoriously unreliable *Steam Packet.*

The town is renowned for its wooden toll swing bridge and fine abbey. Every three hours, the sound of a carillon hymn tune floats out from a monastic church, where worship has continued since Norman times. It was the first great northern monastery built after the Conquest. William's only English-born son, King Henry I, was born here, an unusual distinction for a busy provincial market town. Market day is on Mondays, and there is a cattle market on Fridays.

## (LEEDS)–MICKLEFIELD–YORK

**by John Bushell**

From Micklefield the York line of 1869 descends northwards, joining the 1840 Yorkshire & North Midland line at Church Fenton. To the east, there is a fine view of Sherburn in Elmet's fifteenth-century church. Sherburn was old when the Normans came for the old Celtic 'Kingdom of Elmete' held out against Saxon invaders, and the name survives to this day. The village is served by York–Sheffield trains.

Church Fenton boasts a thirteenth-century church, and an RAF station well known for its annual air display. Until 1964 a line ran towards Tadcaster, Wetherby, and Harrogate.

The four tracks from here onwards prove to be a racecourse over the Plain of York. Most local stations were closed in the 1960s, but Ulleskelf, a popular venue for fishermen, survived. This was largely because of the lack of a direct road to York, for the River Wharfe has no road bridge between Tadcaster and Cawood. The approach to York sees the junction with the new 1983 East Coast main line to Doncaster, at Colton. Before 1871 the main line to Doncaster was via Church Fenton, Knottingley, and the Lancashire & Yorkshire line.

Dringhouses Yard marks the approach to one of our great railway centres, York, headquarters from 1854 of the North Eastern Railway, and today of British Rail Eastern Region. The magnificent offices stand inside the City Wall, beside the original station of 1841.

York is a Mecca for rail enthusiasts. The National Railway Museum is situated in the former engine sheds ½ mile to the north of the station. At busy times, hundreds gather to watch trains on the curving platforms beneath the fine roof span of 1877. Today the occasional 'Scarborough Spa Special' reminds us of a former Golden Age of Steam. In 1900 the North Eastern 'single drivers' would slow through the station on the fast Leeds–Scarborough non-stop service completing the 67½ miles in seventy-five minutes! Today's diesels require about ninety minutes (albeit with three stops).

The North Eastern Railway left its mark in the coat of arms embossed at the top of each Corinthian column of the station's 800-foot-long roof. Those nearest the footbridge are carefully restored. When first opened, Thomas Prosser, the designer, claimed it to be the largest station in Europe. In spite of wartime bombing and modernisation, it survives. The train shed is superb, as is the ornate ironwork, half hidden in the many nooks and crannies. Recent careful restoration includes a Tourist Office, an eighty-year-old glazed NER tile map, and an NER slotted post signal, which adorns the entrance hall. the former tea rooms are now a Rail Riders Model Railway Exhibition.

# A GUIDED WALK ROUND YORK

**by Nigel Cross**

York is one of the finest cities in the North. The rail-traveller today alights close to all the main attractions, the first encountered being the City Wall. The gleaming cream twelfth to fourteenth-century defences have survived virtually complete. Today's tourists find it a traffic-free pedestrian route to Clifford's Tower and the renowned Castle Museum. The whole city is a Conservation Area, the narrow medieval streets being dominated by the majestic Minster, the largest Gothic cathedral in Europe. In the past, perhaps, the 'visitors' were not always welcome. The Romans called it 'Eboracum', the Vikings, 'Jorvik', the Saxons, 'Eferwick'.

The suggested walk is intended to give the visitor a glimpse of some of the city's many attractions. It does not claim to cover everything. Nor does it claim to provide an in-depth knowledge of the sites covered. The walk is designed to whet the visitor's appetite for further exploration. The walk is physically an easy one, but please allow at least half a day as there is a lot to see.

On leaving the station, turn left, past the Royal York Hotel and left again along Leeman Road under the railway bridge to the National Railway Museum, which is fully described below. After leaving the museum, retrace your tracks back under the railway tunnel. On your immediate left, after leaving the tunnel, is a narrow alley between the railway and the Post Office. Take that alley and it will bring you down to the the River Ouse. On your left is Scarborough Railway Bridge, which incorporates a footbridge. Take the bridge across the river. After crossing the Ouse bear right. On your left are the Museum Gardens, a haven from the hustle and bustle that is York. Here among the beautiful gardens, squirrels, peacocks, and other wildlife roam free. Also here are the Yorkshire Museum and the ruins of St Mary's Abbey, which form the backcloth for the York Mystery Plays.

Leave the gardens by the Museum Street Gate and proceed left along Museum Street. On your right you will pass the Assembly Rooms. Continuing straight forward at the set of traffic lights will bring you to the Minster, one of the high points of the walk. Work on this magnificent building started in 1220 or thereabouts, and has never really finished, what with additions, alterations, and renovation work. The main restoration work at the moment, is a result of a fire in July 1984. To appreciate this and other surrounding buildings, you should take a walk around the outside of the

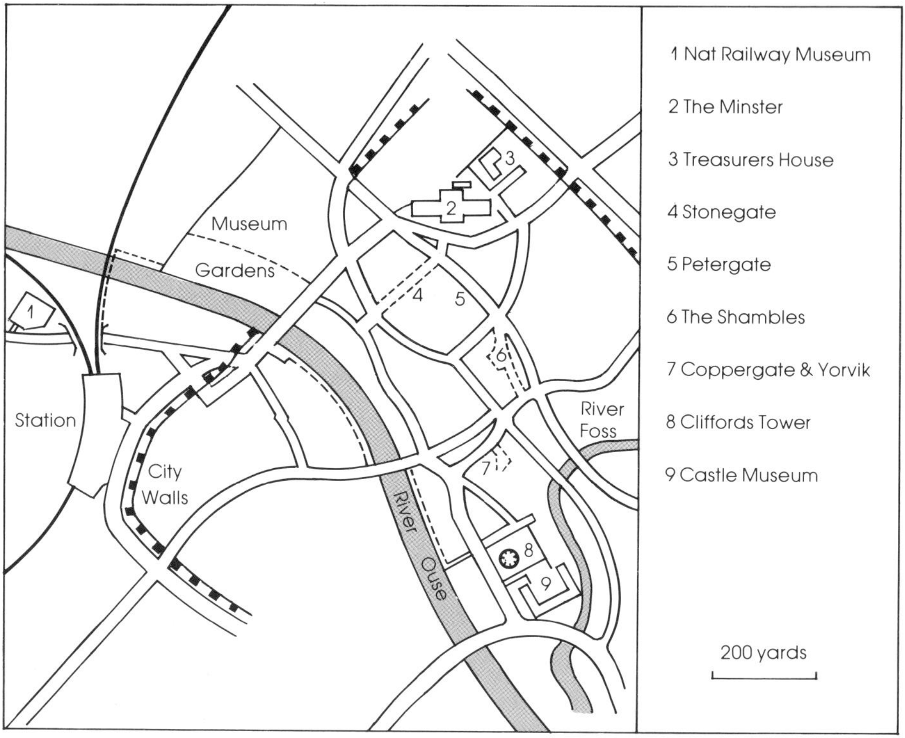


York

Minster, as well as a look inside. A visit to the Crypt is also recommended.

Running parallel with the Minster is Petergate. This, along with Parliament Street, Coney Street, and Stonegate, forms the main shopping area of York. Most of the shops in this area have retained an olde-worlde character, none more so than those along Petergate and Stonegate. If you end up along Parliament Street, try the Roman Bath public house at the corner of St Sampson's Square. It is built over a Roman bath, hence the name. Inside, part of the floor has been cut away to highlight the remains.

If you continue along Petergate to King's Square and then bear right, it will bring you to The Shambles, a beautiful example of a medieval street. The ground floors of the buildings along this street make attractive shops.

At the end of The Shambles, turn right in Stonebow and proceed into Coppergate. Very soon, on your left, you will come to the new Coppergate Centre. Turn into that centre and on your right is the Jorvik Centre. This centre offers a ride back in time to the Viking era. The experience is not just one of sight, but also sound and, rather unusually, smell. A word of warning: if you intend to visit the exhibition, be prepared to queue for up to an hour in the high season. It was while excavating the Coppergate Centre that many Viking remains were found. The old building next to the Jorvik Centre was once a church. It is now one of Britain's largest Heritage Centres.

From the Jorvik centre, follow the signs to the Castle. This should take you to the right of 'Fenwicks' and down a passage. This will lead you to Castle Hill, with Clifford's Tower perched on top. On your left is York's other river, the Foss. Past Castle Hill, the impressive building in the square forms the Castle Museum. The highlight of this museum is the Edwardian street scene.

After visiting this museum, cross Tower Street and head down through the gardens to the River Ouse. If you fancy taking to the water, boat trips leave from here. They also depart from the Mansion House, near Lendal Bridge. Turn right and follow the river bank to Ouse Bridge. By the side of Ouse Bridge is another interesting pub, the King's Arms. This pub is one of York's main flood casualties.

Cross the Ouse Bridge, turn right, and proceed north along the opposite river bank. This is Lendal Walk. You will pass the Viking Hotel. Immediately after passing under Lendal Bridge, turn left up the steps. This will bring you up on to the famous City Walls. Continue along the Walls in a westerly direction. However, do take time to stop and look back; it will give you some superb views of the city. The distinctive building on your left is British Rail's Eastern Region Headquarters. The next building along, behind the Railway War Memorial, hides the fact it was the original railway station in York. By continuing along the Walls, on your right you will pass the present station. Soon you will come to Micklegate Bar. By this point you, or your family, will probably have had enough. Here is an appropriate place to descend from the Walls and return to the railway station, at ground level. The street you need to take is Queen Street. However, before departing Micklegate Bar, allow yourself a few moments to admire one of York's finest gates.

## NATIONAL RAILWAY MUSEUM

**by Ms C. Thornber, Marketing Officer, NRM**

The National Railway Museum in York offers something of interest to every member of the family. The steam railway was invented in Britain and the collection chronicles the whole spectrum of British railway heritage from the earliest horse-drawn vehicles. The museum building was once part of the motive-power depot in York and the main hall retains the atmosphere of the old steam-engine shed. The exhibits are arranged round two turntables; locomotives round one and carriages round the other. Motive power in the collection ranges from the ungainly *Agenoria*, built in 1829 by George Stephenson, to the prototype of British Rail's Experimental Advanced Passenger Train.

The collection of rolling-stock and carriages within the main hall is constantly changing. The easy interchange of rolling-stock by rail is facilitated by the museum's direct rail connection with the British Rail system, a valuable consideration when the collection includes heavy engineering items. This also enables the museum to operate some of its historic rolling-stock and carriages on occasions.

While it is undoubtedly the magnificent display of locomotives and carriages which first catch the visitors eye upon entering the main hall, the museum houses exhibitions covering the many facets of more than 150 years of railways in Britain. On the balcony of the main hall, a wide range of historical material, including timetables, model trains, and railway equipment, tells the story of the social and economic development of British railways. An audio-visual presentation illustrating the varied aspects of railway operations has been prepared by museum staff and is shown in a theatre. The museum also has a fine collection of paintings, photographs, glass, and chinaware which exemplifies the use made by the railways of art and design in their day-to-day business.

In the newly refurbished Buffers Restaurant the visitor can also enjoy an excellent view over the British Rail East Coast main line. The museum is a ten-minute walk from the railway station.

Open weekdays 10 a.m-6 p.m.; Sundays 2.30-6 p.m. Closed Good Friday, May Day Holiday, Christmas Eve, Christmas Day, Boxing Day, New Year's Day.

# 3

# INTO THE EAST RIDING

## SELBY–GILBERDYKE

**by John Dargan**

The railway between Selby and Hull was opened in 1840. Together with the Leeds & Selby Railway, opened six years earlier, it linked Hull to the rest of the country and eventually became part of the North Eastern Railway. Today the line carries a frequent service of trains operating between Hull and Leeds or York, although not all trains call at the intermediate stations.

Leaving Selby we immediately cross the swing bridge over the River Ouse and pass through the local industrial area. The trackbed of the former East Coast main line, used before the Selby diversion was opened in 1983, disappears to the left as we swing eastwards. From here to Brough is the longest stretch of straight track in the country – 18 miles.

As Drax power-station dominates the view to the south, with its clusters of cooling towers and one of the largest chimneys in Europe, we pass the site of Hemingbrough Station closed in 1967. We cannot fail to notice the beautiful slender spire of the parish church, one of the finest in the East Riding. The church dates from the thirteenth century and the spire from the fifteenth. Inside is probably the oldest misericord in the land, reputedly carved about 1200. Hemingbrough is accessible from Selby or our next station, Wressle, but a bicycle is recommended.

Selby swing bridge from the control cabin – the warehouse on the left is the original station
*(Photo: West Yorkshire Transport Museum)*

Just before we enter Wressle we cross over the River Derwent as it passes on its way from the North York Moors to join the River Ouse a couple of miles away. The remains of the fortified manor house, known as 'Wressle Castle', are on our left, built in 1380 by Sir Thomas Percy, one of the famous Earls of Northumberland. It now stands on private land and is not open to the public.

Next is Howden, an historic town famous for its magnificent cruciform minster – one of the largest parish churches in Yorkshire. Built of Tadcaster limestone, it dates mainly from 1267 and the late fourteenth century. It is noted for its tall central tower, ruined choir, roofless chapter-house, and superb fifteenth-century pulpitum. Visitors to the town will find its tourist potential goes almost unnoticed although the Bowman's Hotel, an old coaching inn, maintains the age-old tradition of providing the traveller with good food and hospitality. The station is 1½ miles from the town and is the start of a County Council recreational cycleway taking in 18 miles of local countryside including the site, just to the north of the station, where the airship *R100* was built in the 1920s.

Leaving Howden the distant skyline of Goole is visible as we pass the earthworks of the former Hull & Barnsley Railway, closed in 1959, and reach the local village station of Eastrington. From here we proceed to Staddlethorpe Junction where we join the line from Doncaster.

# DONCASTER – GILBERDYKE – HULL

**by John Dargan**

The first trains ran between Doncaster and Hull, via Goole, in 1869. They used a newly constructed line between Doncaster and Staddlethorpe Junction (Gilberdyke) and then completed the journey to Hull on the existing line, opened in 1840. The section between Doncaster and Thorne was opened by the Manchester, Sheffield & Lincolnshire Railway and the remainder by the North Eastern. Today the line is Hull's main rail artery carrying services to Sheffield, Manchester, Liverpool, and London as well as local services to Goole and Doncaster.

Leaving Doncaster we immediately pass under a road bridge which stands on the site where the Roman road between Lincoln and York passed through the town. Today the bridge carries only local traffic but in bygone days it was part of the Great North Road between London and Edinburgh. Once under it we leave the East Coast main line and swing east towards the flat landscape of the Humberhead marshlands.

For the first few miles we are accompanied by the River Don and its canal. The Etymology of the river is similar to that of the River Danube in Austria; both take their name from the Celtic word *dana* meaning water. The canal dates from 1726 when a series of improvements to the navigation were started which eventually gave the expanding industries of Sheffield and Rotherham an outlet to the River Humber. In recent years further modernisation of this, the Sheffield and South Yorkshire Canal, has taken place in an attempt to rejuvenate the system.

We follow the canal until the industry of Doncaster is almost left behind and the South Yorkshire Joint line, serving pits to the east and south of the town, joins us on the right. As Thorpe Marsh power – station looms on the left, we pass the site of Barnby Dun Station, closed in 1967, and are shortly joined by the West Riding & Grimsby line, which although no longer used by regular passenger trains, once allowed West Riding holiday-makers easy access to the Lincolnshire coast resorts.

Next comes Stainforth and Hatfield Station which serves local mining communities. Hatfield, to the south, was once more famous for its connections with Hatfield Chase where the kings of old had special hunting rights and Edwin the first Christian King of Northumbria was slain by Penda, the pagan King of Mercia in 633. Hatfield Main Colliery is on the left just before we pass under the M18 motorway and leave the Grimsby line at Thorne Junction.

Just before entering Thorne we pass over the Stainforth and Keadby Canal and to our right is Thorne Lock which is being developed as a marina and leisure park. Thorne itself is an ancient market town (market day is Tuesday) and until recently the home of Darley's Brewery. The beer is still available in the town. The town has two stations, Thorne North, on the Hull line, and Thorne South on the line to Grimsby. The town lies midway between the two, which are a good mile apart.

Leaving Thorne we strike out over the broad marshland plain which until the seventeenth century was largely open fen and peatmoss. It was almost devoid of settlement and subject to severe flooding until 1626 when a Dutchman, Cornelius Vermuyden, improved the drainage to such an extent that much of the area is now fertile agricultural land. On a clear day the open spaces allow the eye to wander a distance as Thorpe Marsh, Ferrybridge, Eggborough, and Drax power-stations are all visible. As we pass the recently reopened Thorne Colliery the dockland skyline of Goole appears on the horizon.

Before entering Goole we cross the Dutch River, the Aire and Calder Navigation, and the original line of the former Lancashire & Yorkshire Railway from Wakefield, opened in 1848 and now serving Goole Docks. The connection bringing the present passenger service from Leeds follows shortly on the left. The full range of port activity is now in view and of paticular note are the two distinctive water-towers on the right, the larger of which was once reckoned to be the largest in England. Goole is very much a company creation being built by the Aire and Calder Navigation Company in 1826 and an outlet for the rapidly expanding industry of the West Riding. The main traffic for many years was coal, fed into the port by canal and rail, but today general cargo moved by road is the port's lifeblood. The docks can be viewed at close quarters (just off the High Street) and there is a pleasant walk by the River Ouse where sea-going vessels can sometimes be seen entering or leaving the docks. Market day is Wednesday, when some public houses open all day. A little farther afield (4 miles) is the historic town of Howden with its famous minster church.

A DMU negotiates Goole swing bridge, seen from the air (*Photo: Aerial Photographic Services, Pontefract*)

From Goole we climb slightly to cross the River Ouse. To our left is the tower of Howden Minster, the M62 motorway bridge, and below it the much-dwarfed Boothferry Bridge. We cross the river by the controversial swing bridge built in 1869. When it opened it was the second largest of its type in the world but today many vessels have problems getting safely through its opening span, as the river can be difficult to navigate at this point. As we pass over the river we cross the historic boundary between the West Riding and the East Riding of Yorkshire. For the next few miles we travel though some pleasant unspoiled countryside. Saltmarshe, the next station along, took its name from the local landowner although it actually serves the village of Laxton. Watch out for the majestic cock pheasants strolling along this section of the line and also the beautiful panoramic skies which are a distinctive feature of this area.

At Staddlethorpe Junction we join the line from Leeds and Selby and enter Gilberdyke Station which serves the rapidly expanding commuter population of the village. From here we rise gently and cross over the Market Weighton Canal, completed in 1782. It was built primarily to drain the surrounding area but saw use transporting corn, timber, and coal. A brick and earthenware industry developed along its banks but with the decline in trade the canal was abandoned in 1971. Away to the left the gentle chalk uplands of the Yorkshire Wolds are in evidence as we head towards Broomfleet, a somewhat remote station which serves the small local village. Between Broomfleet and Brough we get our first glimpse of the River Humber and the Wolds of Lincolnshire which lie beyond.

Brough was once the fortified Roman town of Petuaria. It guarded the ferry-crossing used by the Romans on their way between Lincoln and York. Little evidence remains today, however, and most people will associate Brough with Blackburn's aircraft factory sited between the railway and the river. Here flying boats, Beverley Transports, Skuas (the first plane to sink a ship by dive-bombing), and Buccaneers were built. Here also the Wolds sweep down to meet the river and splendid views of the Humber await anyone prepared to venture on to higher ground (fifty-minute walk). In the nearby village of Welton (2 miles) is the Green Dragon Inn where Dick Turpin is said to have been arrested.

The next station is the unadvertised Melton Halt which serves adjacent industry—note the tall smelting-works chimney, a landmark for miles around. A short distance farther and we arrive at the attractive station serving the outer suburban village of North Ferriby. Its name probably derives from the ferry which the local Celtic tribe, the Parisi, used between here and South Ferriby on the far side of the river.

The skies are still very much in evidence as we leave Ferriby and enter one of the most attractive sections of our line. Here the train skirts a broad sweep of the River Humber. On a full tide there is usually plenty of activity in the shipping lanes, while closer to hand the muddy foreshore provides refuge for numerous gulls and wading birds. The eye of most travellers, however, will be fastened on the Humber Bridge which dominates the view. Although of doubtful merit in transportation terms there can be no denying its aesthetic impact as it gracefully stretches out almost 1½ miles to reach the shores of Lincolnshire.

Hessle, our next station, is now little more than an extension of the Hull metropolis although at one time it was well outside its reach. If a walk across the world's largest single-span suspension bridge is desired then this is the place to alight. Barton-on-Humber at the other side is a welcoming little town where the usual sustenance can be obtained and trains to Grimsby can be caught. Hessle is also the start of a pleasant 20-mile walk to Beverley taking in the eastern slopes of the Yorkshire Wolds (the Beverley Twenty), and of the Wolds Way, a long-distance footpath which follows the Wolds to Filey. A similar route, the Viking Way, starts from Barton-on-Humber and follows the Lincolnshire Wolds.

Leaving Hessle we pass through the site of the massive Priory Yard sidings, now derelict and awaiting redevelopment. To our right is the Clive Sullivan Way, a dual carriageway named after a local rugby player. British Rail still retains a foothold in the area and we shortly pass the Speedlink and Freightliner terminals and, on the right, Tilcon's aggregate depot. Beyond Tilcon lies St Andrew's Dock, once one of the country's premier fish docks, but now disused, as what little fish enters Hull, mainly by road from Bridlington and Aberdeen, is handled at the nearby Albert Dock. Also on the right, the former Dairycoates locomotive shed, once the largest in the land, is now used as a container depot while on the left a line diverges from ours and after serving Hull City Football Ground, seen in the near distance, heads for King George Dock and the chemical complex at Saltend. We then pass Anlaby Road Circle Cricket Ground, where Yorkshire occasionally play, the junction with the Scarborough line and the Hull Royal Infirmary before finally coming to rest in Hull Paragon Station below William Bell's splendid roof built in 1904.

# HULL

**by John Dargan**

Kingston upon Hull came into existence in the twelfth century. It quickly developed and by the Middle Ages had become strategically important enough to be protected by fortified walls and a moat. It continued to expand in the eighteenth and nineteenth centuries, eventually becoming a major commercial seaport and one of the world's largest fishing ports. Today only King George Dock remains of any importance, although the city still relies heavily on the river for its lifeblood.

The 'old town', which formerly lay behind the city walls, is the most interesting area for the visitor. To reach it, cross the road outside the main station entrance and go down Jameson Street, turning right into King Edward Street and Queen Victoria Square. Here stands the imposing Dock office building, now the Town Docks Museum. It contains an impressive collection of items associated with Hull's maritime history, particularly the trawling and whaling industries. Past the museum is Whitefriargate which marks the entrance to the 'old town'.

One of the main places of interest is the house in High Street where the city's most famous son, William Wilberforce, was born in 1759. He was largely responsible for the abolition of the slave-trade, and inside can be found some of his personal mementoes and an intersting display of slave-trade relics. Also in High Street is the Black Boy, an historic public house associated with cock-fighting and press-gangs. Hull's most famous pub, however, is Ye Olde White Hart, off Silver Street. Here in 1642 the decision was taken to refuse King Charles I entry to the town, thus declaring Hull's Civil War sympathies to lie with Parliament. Another interesting pub is the George Inn, down the curiously named Land of Green Ginger. In its walls is 'the smallest window in the country', allegedly used to warn customers of approaching press-gangs.

In the Market Place is the Old Grammar School, built in 1583, and the largest parish church in the country—Holy Trinity. It is an outstanding example of fourteenth-century architecture and contains some of the earliest known English brickwork. A short walk from the Market Place is Victoria Pier fronting the River Humber. Until 1981 the home of the Humber Ferries, it is now a popular place to watch the activity on the river—perhaps from the Minerva Hotel, once the haunt of whaling captains talking of voyages to the icy waters of Greenland, but now better known for its home-brewed Pilots Pride. Close by are the former Town Docks which have found new use as an attractive yachting marina.

# 4

# THE YORKSHIRE COAST

## HULL–SCARBOROUGH

**by John Dargan**

The lines between Hull and Bridlington, and Filey and Seamer Junction were opened in 1846 followed by the 'missing' middle section a year later. At Seamer Junction connection was made with the York–Scarborough line opened in 1845, both lines eventually becoming part of the North Eastern Railway. Today the line carries a regular service of local trains supplemented by holiday excursion traffic during the summer months.

Our exit from Hull takes us past the Royal Infirmary and the junction with the line to Doncaster and Leeds. To the left a little farther along is Walton Street, the site of Hull's famous fair held each year in October, and to the right Hymer's College and Spring Bank Cemetery, where many of the 1,800 victims of Hull's cholera outbreak in 1849 lie buried. We then pass under the freight line which serves King George Dock and the chemical complex at Saltend.

Our first call is at Cottingham, once the largest village in England, but now little more than a pleasant extremity of Hull's metropolis and a dormitory for its University. The site of Baynard Castle where Edward I stayed in 1293 can still be identified but Skidby Windmill (2 miles) is of more interest. Built in 1821, it has recently been restored to working order and now houses a museum of milling agriculture.

A few minutes later our approach to the market town of Beverley is dominated by its famous Minster. Dating from 1220 it is one of the most charming examples of Gothic architecture in Europe, being particularly noted for its two magnificent west towers. Inside is the 1,000-year-old Fridstol, once used by fugitives seeking sanctuary, and the fourteenth-century Percy Tomb–a triumph of medieval art. The town itself is very historic, with much to offer the visitor including the North Bar medieval gateway, the Museum of Army Transport, and the Westwood, over 500 acres of open pasture and common parkland. St Mary's Church, dating from 1120, is also notable with its magnificent west front and beautiful chancel ceiling. Inside is a carved rabbit said to be the model for the White Rabbit in *Alice's Adventures in Wonderland*. Markets are held on Wednesdays and Saturdays when visitors can be recommended to the Beverley Arms, an historic coaching inn reputedly used by Dick Turpin, and the seventeenth-century White Horse–known universally as 'Nellies'–where a more rustic atmosphere may be enjoyed.

From Beverley the train begins to skirt the Yorkshire Wolds as we head north past the former RAF Leconfield. It is now the Army's Normandy Barracks but is still used by the RAF's North Sea Helicopter Rescue Service. Arram is the local station, after which the line runs through the flat, featureless landscape of open farmland and dykes, so characteristic of the Holderness Plain. In the distance, above the Wolds, the tall slender spire of South Dalton Church can be seen, a useful guide for the traveller in an area otherwise devoid of notable landmarks.

The village station of Hutton Cranswick is next, after which we cross a tributary of the River Hull and enter Driffield. Known locally as the 'Capital of the Wolds', history seems to have largely passed it by, although the remains of ancient settlements abound on the nearby Wolds and legend has it that Alfred the Great is buried here. Today the town is chiefly an agricultural centre for the surrounding corn-growing region but it is also an ideal base from which to explore the Wolds, with Sledmere House (7 miles) and Burton Agnes Hall (6 miles) within easy cycling distance. A short walk from the station is the head of Driffield Canal, where ghosts of the town's industrial past still linger. It was opened in 1770 to handle the area's agricultural produce and closed in the 1950s.

Nafferton, our next station, probably takes its name from the spings which occasionally bubble up from the chalk bedrock and are known locally as 'naffers'. It is an interesting 'street' village with many reminders of its agricultural roots, including the Station Mills built in 1860 and the former Maltings built in 1840. The land begins to undulate slightly as a few miles farther on we pass Burton Agnes Hall on our left. Built in red brick, it is one of the North of England's finest Elizabethan mansion houses, containing some magnificent wood carving and plasterwork, as well as a fine collection of paintings.

The sight of industry to our right heralds the approach to Bridlington, one of Yorkshire's most popular holiday resorts. It stands astride the Gypsey Race, a spring that rises in the Wolds and flows through the town into the North Sea. The beach and usual seaside entertainments can be found down by the ancient quay and harbour, where the colourful fishing fleet can usually be seen. From here splendid views of Bridlington Bay may be enjoyed or advantage taken of one of the many boat trips on offer. Farther inland is the 'old market town' where the remains of an Augustine priory dating from 1120 are to be found. Although most of it has been destroyed, the beautiful nave has survived as the parish church. It has a magnificent 55-foot-high west window, considered to be one of the finest in the country, while near by is the Bayle Gate built about 1390 and once the priory's gatehouse.

Shortly after leaving Bridlington we get our first rooftop glimpse of the sea and the cliffs of Flamborough. The train begins to climb as it cuts through the chalk headland and reaches Bempton. From here it is only 3 miles to Flamborough village where St Oswald's Church contains a striking sixteenth-century rood-screen and a memorial to Sir Marmaduke Constable who died in 1520 after reputedly being consumed from within by a toad which he had accidentally swallowed! The main attraction, however, is Flamborough Head, with its impressive 200-foot-high cliffs, numerous colonies of seabirds, and spectacular views over the North Sea. Its lighthouse, built in 1806, stands dominant as it warns shipping away from the treacherous rocks which lie below. Visitors should also visit Danes Dyke, a massive 2½-mile-long entrenchment which bisects the headland and probably dates from the Iron Age. Bempton itself is famous for its sheer 400-foot-high cliffs where the gannet has its only mainland nesting site. Until quite recently some of the local people, known as 'climmers', used to lower themselves over the cliff edge in baskets to harvest the vast quantity of seabirds' eggs. Times change, however, and the cliffs are now a bird sanctuary. There is excellent clifftop walking in this area.

From Bempton we continue to cut through the chalk, with the sea out of sight but never very far away. We turn inland slightly and reach the village of Hunmanby, pleasantly situated where the Wolds sweep down towards the sea. In former days it was of some importance with its regular markets and fairs, and the medieval Market Cross can still be seen close to the main street. Earlier still it is thought to have been the site of a Bronze Age settlement as a 'chariot burial' was discovered near by. In the 2 miles separating the village from the coast, Billy Butlin established his Filey Holiday Camp, and today the fine sandy beaches continue to attract holiday-makers, many of whom now use the area's numerous caravan sites.

As we leave Hunmanby we pass the trackbed of the branch line which until 1976

Scarborough beach and town with castle beyond *(Photo: Mike Crowhurst)*

served Butlin's Filey Holiday Camp. The sea is once more in view and the cliffs of Bempton and Flamborough can be seen to the rear. A short distance farther and we enter Filey Station, which still retains its over-all roof, once a common feature of many East Riding stations. Originally Filey was a quiet fishing community and it was not until Victorian times that it developed as a fashionable holiday resort. It never achieved the popularity of its larger neighbours, however, and still retains its relatively peaceful atmosphere, with its long promenade and vast expanse of fine pebble-free sands. Fishing still plays a part in the town's economy and the clifftop Church of St Oswald has an interesting window commemorating local fishermen who have been lost at sea. To the north of the town is Filey Brigg, a mile-long spur of oolitic rock which juts out into the bay and provides an adventurous stroll for many a summer-time holiday-maker.

From Filey the train turns inland again and passes the sites of Gristhorpe and Cayton stations, closed in the 1950s. The sea is lost to view, but across the open countryside the steep slopes of Staxton mark the northern extremity of the Wolds. At Seamer Junction we join the line from York and enter Seamer Station, which serves an area now almost part of suburban Scarborough.

From Seamer it is only a couple of miles to the 'Queen of Watering Places' as Scarborough likes to style itself. Originally famous for its medicinal spa waters discovered in 1626, it is now one of the country's premier resorts, offering an interesting variety of holiday attractions. As we approach the town we pass Oliver's Mount with its obelisk commemorating those who died in the First World War, while across the rooftops we can see the ruins of Scarborough Castle. Other than this the resort remains largely unseen from the train and only a venture down towards the bay will reveal its seaside delights!

## YORK – SCARBOROUGH

**by John Bushell**

Leaving York towards the north, the Scarborough line immediately crosses the River Ouse, affording an attractive view of the Lendal road bridge to the south, alongside it St Leonard's Tower, and in summer a whole flotilla of pleasure-craft. Close to the railway bridge in the last century was Duff Jetty, where barges received the contents of rail wagons, called 'duff' – small coals to be transported to the York Glassworks. A most spectacular accident took place a little over a century ago, when a coupling broke and twenty wagons followed one another straight into the river, the last four remaining above the water!

On the eastern bank are the remains of St Mary's Abbey, within the Museum Gardens, which were laid out as botanical gardens early in the nineteenth century. Today, peacocks strut through the mature woodland, but little remains of what was the most important Benedictine abbey in the eleventh and twelfth centuries. It was from here in 1132 that thirteen monks walked out because of 'lax standards' and founded the Cistercian Fountains Abbey, near Ripon. After dissolution in the sixteenth century, the remains became a quarry, stone being used in York Prison and even as far afield as Beverley Minster. What remains serves as an attractive backcloth for the York Mystery Plays.

The junction to the south links the main-line system to two unusual destinations. The first, Rowntrees' chocolate factory, sees both goods and special passenger train service for the workers only, to the company's own Rowntrees Halt. The second links up with Derwent Valley Light Railway, one of the few railway companies that escaped both Grouping and Nationalisation. Passenger services from York (Layerthorpe) to Cliff Common Near Selby ran from 1913 to just 1926. Freight business has now contracted to shunting operations within the Layerthorpe goods depot. There is, however, talk of reopening a short section at Murton, as part of the developing Yorkshire Museum of Farming.

On leaving the city, the direct York-Hull line diverged, to serve Pocklington, Market Weighton, and Beverley. Although in 1849 a shareholder described it as a 'beautifully made line but, unfortunately, without passengers to travel on it!', it survived until the Beeching Age, closing to all traffic on 29 November 1965. Today the through York – Hull trains run via the new line and Hambleton Junction to Selby.

Many of the wayside stations on the York – Scarborough line survive as private dwellings, the twelve intermediate stops having closed to passengers on 22 September 1930. This was part of a scheme to provide a co-ordinated service, with the part-railway-owned West Yorkshire Road Car Company operating a station-to-station bus link from York and Malton to Scarborough. This in turn relieved pressure on the main-line holiday trains, which in summer were unbelievably frequent. A train every six minutes was normal at busy times.

The 42-mile line itself is quite level in spite of crossing the Howardian Hills. Earlier plans to tunnel for 1,430 yards were replaced by the present tortuous line, following the River Derwent. This added 1¾ miles and means a 40 mph restriction for 3¾ miles. Loss in time is more than compensated with one of the country's most scenic journeys.

Yorkshire's River Derwent unusually starts just 8 miles from the sea, on the North York Moors, and then flows inland for 70 miles before joining the Ouse, the Humber, and finally the North Sea. Originally it flowed into the sea at Scarborough, but during the Ice Age the Vale of Pickering became a giant lake, and the river carved for itself a gorge to enable it to flow inland. The railway uses this easy route, joining the river 1½ miles beyond Barton Hill, where the A64 Leeds – Scarborough road crosses. Three miles south of this point is Scrayingham, where George Hudson, 'The Railway King', lies buried. One-time draper, Lord Mayor of York, and MP for Sunderland, shady dealings in railway finances led to his downfall and disgrace. He died in 1871.

As the train slows for the giant S-bend, we reach, on the right, Kirkham Priory, founded about 1125. The weir on the Derwent was originally a lock, for at one time navigation was possible beyond Malton. The imposing remains of Castle Howard Station remind us that Queen Victoria alighted here one day in 1850, on her way to open the Royal Border Bridge at Berwick and Newcastle's Central Station. Three miles northwards is the ancestral home of the Howards, an attractive eighteenth-century house, replacing an earlier castle, which formed the backcloth for the popular television production of *Brideshead Revisited*. It is open to the public, and the agile will find a good day's walking on the footpaths linking Malton Station with the house (10miles return). A bus service runs along the main road.

Malton (North Riding) Station is in Norton (East Riding), though effectively it is now one town. Malton bustles on market days (Friday and Saturday). At Old Malton (1 mile) stands the historic Abbey. At one time, the NER regarded Malton as an important junction, but the closure of the routes to Driffield (1950), Pilmoor and Gilling (1930), and Pickering for Whitby (1965) means that those who change today rely upon infrequent bus services. The bus station adjoins the railway station. Would-be travellers to Whitby on the North York Moors Railway are advised to check up on services before travelling.

Rillington was the junction for Whitby. The line now runs at the foot of the chalk Yorkshire Wolds (south) while affording distant views of the North Yorkshire Moors. The train speeds on through the closed stations of Knapton, Heslerton, Weaverthorpe, and Ganton. Seamer, the final halt, is today the junction for Filey, Bridlington, and Hull. The line from the north-west (Pickering) closed in 1950; this served the popular beauty-spots of Forge Valley and Thornton Dale.

The final 3 miles into Scarborough Central Station takes us alongside the Mere (right) where children still sail to 'Treasure Island' on the *Hispaniola*. Towering above is Oliver's Mount, 500 feet above sea-level, and offering a panoramic view of the town—though nobody really believes that Oliver Cromwell camped on the top. Londesborough Road Excursion Station (closed) is on the right.

When the railway arrived in 1845, the small fishing port 'had no wish for a great influx of vagrants'. Nevertheless it triggered the development of the Queen of Watering Places. The impressive castle sits high on a promontory between two bays. In the south, the fishing-boats and crab stalls stand close to every kind of amusement. History in the form of King Richard's house and the old parish church, vies with video games in this resort for all tastes. At the foot of the South Cliff is the spa. The North Bay relies more upon the natural attractions of the golden sands. Rail enthusiasts will want to visit England's longest municipal narrow-gauge railway, linking Northstead Manor Gardens to Sealby Mills, using fifty-year-old steam-outline diesel locomotives. Scarborough has attractions for all ages, and has endeavoured to encourage rail travel, by subsidising the provision of a turntable for steam locomotives. Long may this continue.

Today Scarborough is a terminal station, but until 1965 there was a somewhat awkward reversal procedure to gain access to Gannow's Close Tunnel for the line to Whitby. The route according to the original official guide 'runs through pleasant undulating pasture lands at either end, winds in and out amongst gorse and heather clad hills, dips into wooded dales, skirts the edge of a wild moor, climbs to the highest cliff on the Yorkshire Coast, runs round one of the bonniest bays in the Kingdom, and perches on the brow of a cliff against which the waves ceaselessly break'. Alas, the delights of such a 23½-mile rail journey are but a memory. In spite of the promises of survival from the Prime Minister, Harold Wilson (at election time), and warnings from the Transport Users' Consultative Committee of severe hardship, the route closed on 6 March 1965. Today there are some alternative United Bus services available. Where steam-engines once laboured up the 1 in 41 gradient from attractive Robin Hood's Bay to bleak Ravenscar, nothing disturbs the peace and beauty today, other than the tramp of heavy boots, for this section is now a popular footpath. For the walker who loves old railways, this area is a must, and can be reached quite easily from either the Scarborough or Whitby railheads.

# 5

# HARROGATE AND KNARESBOROUGH

## LEEDS–HARROGATE–YORK

**by James Rogers**

Prior to 1967, many trains between Leeds and Harrogate ran to or from the North, via Ripon and Northallerton. Although there were a few trains between Leeds and Knaresborough, most trains on the York branch ran between Harrogate and York. It was only after passenger trains were withrawn from the Harrogate–Ripon–Northallerton line in 1967 that a regular Leeds Harrogate–York through service was introduced. However, although advertised as a through service, passengers between Leeds and York are expected to travel the shorter, cheaper route via Church Fenton. for this reason, trains for York via Harrogate are advertised, at Leeds, as travelling only as far as Poppleton, and at York as travelling only as far as Headingley. Passengers travelling between the two cities via Harrogate may be asked to pay a higher fare. With the exception of Harrogate, all intermediate stations on the Leeds–Harrogate–York line are unstaffed and trains have conductor guards.

For about a mile after leaving Leeds, Harrogate trains follow the same route as that by trains for Ilkley, Skipton, and the north-west but, on approaching Armley Prison, the large castle-like building on the left, turn sharply right and cross the Leeds and Liverpool Canal, the River Aire, and the Kirkstall Road by means of the twenty-three-arch Aire Viaduct. One of the first travellers over this viaduct, in 1849, noted that the spires and chimneys of Leeds could be seen in the distance, but the suburbs of Leeds have long since absorbed the viaduct. In the 1840s there existed on the right near the Headingley end of the viaduct, the Leeds Zoological and Botanic Gardens. Unfortunately, despite being a popular destination for Leeds people, with its own station, the gardens were soon developed for housing and all that now remains is a bear pit, not visible from the train. The station, too, has also long since disappeared.

After passing through the short St Anne's Tunnel, Headingley Station is reached. The early station building, with its low platform, can be seen on the left. Trains arriving at Headingley today use staggered platforms of normal height. Headingley is famous for cricket. Maps giving directions to the cricket ground are exhibited at the station, but in case of difficulty passengers should leave the station on the same side as the station buildings and turn left into Kirkstall Lane. The cricket ground is on the right, just over ½ mile from the station.

Kirkstall Abbey can also be reached from Headingley Station. Leave the station on the same side as the station buildings, turn right into Kirkstall Lane, then right into Abbey Road. The abbey is on the left, almost a mile from the station. Founded in 1152 it was reduced to ruins after the Dissolution of the Monasteries in 1539. The medieval gatehouse is now a folk museum and includes full-size Victorian streets of shops and cottages, complete with period interiors. Leaving Headingley, passengers can glimpse the abbey's ruined tower above houses on the left. The line then continues

Montpellier Gardens, Harrogate, with the townsfolk enjoying the sunshine *(Photo: Harrogate Borough Council)*

over the Leeds ring road and through Clayton Wood, passing on the right an extensive quarry, to reach Horsforth.

On leaving Horsforth the Leeds suburbs are left behind and soon Bramhope Tunnel is entered. This tunnel, named after the village under which it passes, is 2 miles 241 yards long, the sixth longest on British Rail. Its construction, between 1845 and 1849, proved extremely difficult, mainly because of the huge inflow of water – no less than 1,563,480,000 gallons poured in. At least nineteen shafts were sunk to assist construction, four of which remain as air shafts. The tunnel's northern portal is castellated, and features the arms of the Leeds & Thirsk Railway Company, which built the tunnel and, carved in stone, the face of a man. The face of a different man is featured on the southern portal. A memorial, in the shape of the tunnel's northern portal, to those who died in the tunnel's construction stands in the churchyard at Otley.

Shortly after Bramhope Tunnel the remains of the disused Arthington Station are passed. This station closed in 1965, along with the Arthington – Otley line. The abandoned route of the Otley line can be seen branching off on the left, and is a reminder that some Leeds – Ilkley trains once took this route.

After Arthington, a viaduct of twenty-one arches over the River Wharfe is crossed. This affords an excellent view of the surrounding countryside, whether to the left up the Wharfe Valley towards Pool, or to the right towards Harewood. A long, high embankment is followed by the short Castley Tunnel and then Weeton Station, which is made almost entirely of wood, and is actually in Huby. The Great Alms Cliff, also known as Almscliff Crag, a local landmark over 700 feet above sea-level, can be reached on foot from Weeton Station. The panoramic view from the top is well worth the walk. In 1766 a young girl threw herself from the top but a strong wind caused her dress to act as a parachute and she floated safely to the ground and lived to an old age. On leaving the station turn right into the main Pool – Harrogate road, then turn left into Crag Lane. A footpath leads from this lane to the cliff.

The next station after Weeton is Pannal. Here the station buildings have been converted into a public house called 'Platform One', and a Pullman car originally Car No. 332 but now named 'Mae', acts as a restaurant. On leaving Pannal the Crimple Viaduct of thirty-one arches can be seen on the left. This was completed in 1848 to carry the York & North Midland Railway's Church Fenton – Harrogate line. The line between Leeds and Pannal was opened throughout in 1849 as part of the Leeds & Thirsk Railway. from Pannal this railway ran north through Crimple Valley, avoiding Harrogate, to a station at Starbeck and then proceeded to Thirsk, and later Northallerton, via Ripon. That part of the line between Pannal Junction and Starbeck was abandoned in 1951. In 1862 a short connecting line was built from what was to be Pannal Junction to the south end of Crimple Viaduct, and it is this line that the Leeds–Harrogate trains use today. A sharp curve brings trains on to the viaduct at what used to be Crimple Junction. On the right trees and shrubs now hide the abandoned route from Church Fenton. Until its closure in 1964 part of the Church Fenton–Harrogate line was used by Leeds–Wetherby–Harrogate trains. Crossing Crimple Viaduct the abandoned route of the Leeds & Thirsk Railway can be seen running underneath and on the right the viaduct of seven arches which carried the line over the River Crimple. Also visible on the right, in the distance, is the site where each July is held the Great Yorkshire Show.

From the end of Crimple Viaduct the line to Harrogate runs mainly through cuttings but on approaching Harrogate sharp-eyed passengers may glimpse, branching off to the left, the original route of the Church Fenton line, which reached its Harrogate terminus, called Brunswick after a nearby hotel, through a tunnel. Both tunnel and terminus were abandoned as long ago as the 1860s when a new line, over which the train now travels, was opened through central Harrogate. A plaque on the Stray, in front of Trinity Church, marks the site of Brunswick Station.

Part of the Stray, Harrogate's famous parkland, can be seen on the approach to the town and on the left a dome-like structure supported by pillars can be glimpsed. This is the Tewit Well, one of the famous mineral springs on which the prosperity of the town was founded. Although they no longer come to take the waters, visitors to Harrogate are still numerous. The town, now one of Britain's leading conference centres, has managed to move with the times but still keep much of its Victorian atmoshphere. With the exception of the railway station, which was rebuilt in the mid 1960s, the town centre has escaped the massive redevelopments experienced by other towns in the post-war years. Harrogate, famous for its parks and gardens, especially the Valley Gardens in which major flower shows are held, has won many awards, both British and European, as a floral town. The town's bus station stands next to the railway station, and did so long before the word 'interchange' became fashionable. From here frequent buses run to Ripon and Pateley Bridge, places once served by rail.

On leaving Harrogate the line drops sharply down a 1 in 66 gradient, passing on the right an Asda supermarket, built on the site of the old goods yard. A little farther on, the site of the former Dragon Junction is passed. Here the now-abandoned line to Ripon and the North branched off to the left and ran down to Bilton Junction, about ¼ mile away, where it joined the original Leeds–Thirsk line. At Dragon the York line curves sharply to the right and soon passes on the left a small reservoir, built to supply the railway with water. On the other side of this reservoir ran the Starbeck-Bilton section of the Leeds–Thirsk line, which at Starbeck North formed a junction with the Harrogate–York line.

Starbeck was once an important railway centre. At one time there stood on the right of the station a large goods yard complete with warehouses and cattle dock, but houses now occupy the site. Once over the level crossing at the end of the station, the site of Starbeck locomotive shed and marshalling yard, both closed in 1959, comes into view on the right. The Leeds–Thirsk line from Pannal approached Starbeck through the centre of this yard. Part of the site is now occupied by the Great Yorkshire Railway Preservation Society, who have a small collection of locomotives and rolling-stock in their care.

The line next runs through a wooded cutting and crosses the River Nidd by what is probably the most-photographed railway viaduct in Britain. On the right, high above the river, stands Knaresborough Castle, a ruin since the Civil War. In the castle grounds a museum illustrates the town's history. The cave of Mother Shipton, Knaresborough's famous prophetess, and the Dropping, or Petrifying, Well, where suspended objects are 'turned to stone', can be visited on the Starbeck side of the Nidd. Also worth a visit is the House in the Rock, also called Fort Montague, which was carved out of the living rock between 1770 and 1786. Knaresborough is a market town, the market being held each Wednesday. The railway station is unstaffed but the station buildings have been converted into shops, and a restaurant called 'Off the Rails'.

The line from Starbeck to Knaresborough was built as a branch of the Leeds & Thirsk Railway while the line from Knaresborough to York was built by the East & West Yorkshire Junction Railway and opened in 1848, although until 1851, when the viaduct was completed, trains to York started from a temporary station about 1 mile east of the present one. York-bound trains leave Knaresborough through a short tunnel and soon after emerging pass, on the left, the abandoned route to Boroughbridge and Pilmoor. This branch, which joined the East Coast main line at Pilmoor, lost its passenger service in 1950 and closed completely in 1964.

From Knaresborough to Cattal the York line has been reduced to single track, as an economy measure. Almost 3 miles from Knaresborough the remains of the closed Goldsborough Station are passed. At the end of the platform on the left stands a disused signal-box built during the Second World War, along with a cold-storage depot, also on the left. In the 1920s the station was often used by royalty, for Princess Mary, the daughter of King George V and Queen Mary, lived at Goldsborough Hall, just visible in the distance on the right and now a nursing home.

The line from Leeds to Harrogate, with its great tunnel and viaducts, has only one level crossing, at Rigton, but the line from Harrogate to York, after Knaresborough, runs through comparatively flat country with numerous level crossings. Within 2 miles of Goldsborough is another disused station. This is, or was, Hopperton, which until 1925 was called Allerton, and was situated next to the Great North Road. It seems hardly believable today but as late as 1962, when a flyover was built, a level crossing halted all traffic on the road to allow trains to pass. On the left, next to a portion of the Great North Road bypassed by the flyover, stands New Inn Farm, once a coaching inn where mail coaches used to stop to change horses.

The next station is Cattal, happily still open. As the train enters the station it crosses Rudgate, once a Roman road running north from near Tadcaster. From Cattal the line is double until the next station, Hammerton, where it reverts to single track and crosses the River Nidd once more, although at a much lower level than at Knaresborough. Soon the remains of the closed Marston Moor Station are passed. Just over a mile to the right is the site of the Battle of Marston Moor, the biggest battle ever fought in Britain. Here on 2 July 1644, during the Civil War, the Parliamentary army, which had been besieging York, defeated the Royalist army. Cromwell, who took part, was wounded. The Royalist commander, Prince Rupert, escaped after the battle by hiding in a bean field.

A mile from Marston Moor there is a military depot. This, with a small oil terminal between Harrogate and Starbeck, provides the Leeds–Harrogate–York line with its only goods traffic. Hessay Station, which immediately follows the military depot, was closed in September 1958, along with Goldsborough, Hopperton, and Marston Moor. A small BR nursery, which supplies the railway with flowers for its offices and ceremonial occasions, precedes Poppleton, a suburb of York complete with village green and maypole.

From Poppleton the line, once again double track, runs under the recently constructed bypass to join the East Coast main line at Skelton Junction. The main line is then used for the final 2 miles to York. On the right, immediately after passing York Yard North signal-box, is Poppleton Road School, rebuilt after receiving a direct hit from a German bomb in 1942. Also on the right, on the approach to the station, is the National Railway Museum.

# 6

# TWO LINES TO PONTEFRACT

## THE 'FIVE TOWNS'

The area which now forms the eastern part of the Metropolitan District of Wakefield, and which consists predominantly of a number of small towns and mining villages, is known as the 'Five Towns' – Normanton, Castleford, Pontefract, Knottingley, and Featherstone. Normanton, once the Yorkshire equivalent of Crewe, is today served only by the Sheffield – Leeds local service (see Chapter 8), while Featherstone no longer has a passenger service. Pontefract, on the other hand, has been lucky enough to retain two railway stations (although no longer a connection between them), and is thus the focal point of the area in railway terms today.

## LEEDS TO GOOLE

**by David Pickersgill**

Leaving Leeds Station the train eases its way round a sharp curve, passes Holbeck locomotive depot, and enters a series of cuttings through the industrial suburbs of Hunslet and Stourton. This is the former Midland Railway main line, once part of a trunk route from London to Scotland, but now, like far too many other lines in the area, under threat of closure due to fierce restrictions on public transport spending. At present this line has an hourly service from Leeds to Castleford, with twelve trains continuing to Knottingley and five to Goole. There is no Sunday service. In 1985 West Yorkshire County Council proposed that trains between Leeds and Castleford should be diverted via Wakefield, but the line's supporters put up a tremendous fight to prevent this happening, and the policy has now been overturned by the new West Yorkshire P.T.A.

The Hunslet area is noted for its engineering works, particularly the construction of locomotives; such names as Hudswell Clarke, Fowler and, indeed, Hunslet were known in many parts of the world. This tradition is maintained by the last-named company and by the Middleton Railway, where several local products are preserved. One of the earliest lines in the world, dating from 1758, a description of the Middleton Railway can be found in Chapter 1. The works of the Hunslet Company are on the left a couple of miles out of Leeds; at the same point a pair of rusting, weed-grown tracks point to the site of Hunslet Lane, the original terminus of the North Midland Railway, opened in 1840. When the present route into the centre of Leeds was opened, Hunslet Lane became a goods depot and continued in this role until 1970 and closure; its site now stands derelict with only the battered shell of a signal-box standing forlornly among the weeds.

After passing the city's modern-day freight facilities at Hunslet Yard and Stourton container terminal, we leave behind the suburbs in exchange for a countryside of sorts; scenery dominated by Skelton Grange power-station and the scars of open-cast mining.

Across the valley Temple Newsam can be seen on the hilltop, an impressive Tudor mansion owned by Leeds City Council as a museum and public park. Eventually it is hoped to restore the whole area between there and the railway for recreational use when the coal-seams are exhausted.

The first stop is at Woodlesford, after which the line runs through open countryside alongside the River Aire until Methley is reached. At Methley Junction the train diverges from the main line on a branch of the former North Eastern Railway, crosses the River Calder alongside a golf-course reclaimed from a colliery spoil heap, and then joins the Normanton-York line at Whitwood Junction for the short run to Castleford.

Castleford is a town with a long history but, sadly, little to show for it. Its origins date from Roman times when a fort was established to guard a river crossing on the highway from Doncaster to Tadcaster; around this fort, at the confluence of the rivers Calder and Aire, grew the settlement of Lagentium. The area adjacent to the station was excavated in the 1970s and much of the civilian settlement was revealed; finds from this and other local sites are displayed in the town museum, above the library in Carlton Street. Modern Castleford is almost entirely a product of the Industrial Revolution, with mining, glass-making and chemicals its chief industries then and, to a lesser extent, today. It has few historical buildings, the town centre being a hotch-potch of Victorian and later styles, though large-scale redevelopment is likely to change this in the near future.

The town's chief claim to fame is as the birthplace of the sculptor, Henry Moore. A bronze reclining figure, presented to the town by Moore in 1981, can be seen outside the Civic Centre in Ferrybridge Road, about twenty minutes' walk from the station. To many people, however, the name Castleford is synonymous with Rugby League; as a breeding ground for talented players the area has few equals, even if this is not always reflected in the fortunes of the local club!

The main line to the north through Castleford only sees passenger services, to Scarborough, in the summer months; instead our train reverses and diverges to the left round a sharp curve, heading for Pontefract. Between the two towns the line passes scenes of quite spectacular industrial dereliction: collieries, spoil heaps, open-cast pits, and slurry ponds. Pontefract Racecourse is also to be seen to the right of the line; its meetings are very popular with local people in the flat season. As we approach Pontefract Monkhill Station, the train joins the former Lancashire & Yorkshire Railway Wakefield–Goole main line which for almost 150 years has been an artery for vast amounts of coal traffic; formerly to Goole or Hull for shipment, and now to the power-stations sited along the lower reaches of the River Aire. At one time, too, the L & Y's Liverpool–Hull expresses passed this way, but in 1967 the line was closed to passengers, leaving Featherstone and Sharlston without a service. On the wooded hillside to the right stand the ruins of Pontefract Castle; it is well worth a couple of hours' break to explore these and the rest of this interesting town, the attractions of which are fully described in the Sheffield–York section which follows.

Leaving Pontefract we pass alongside modern housing estates overshadowed by the twin chimneys and cooling towers of Ferrybridge power-station. The single track branching off to the left at this point was built in the 1960s to allow coal trains access to the power-station. Soon the train passes over the Sheffield–York line, then the Great North Road, before slowing to a halt at Knottingley. Here is the centre of the railway operation that keeps the power-stations supplied; there are extensive sidings, a modern locomotive maintenance depot, and every few minutes another train rumbling through with up to a thousand tons of coal for the hungry furnaces. The town itself–'Knottla' to the locals–is an uncomfortable mixture of old stone houses and sprawling modern estates. It manufactures glass bottles by the million and boasts one of the few yards still building and repairing canal craft.

The freight railway: a train leaves Eggborough power-station after delivering its load of coal *(Photo: David Thurlow)*

Eastwards from Knottingley the line runs across the broad plain that stretches south from the Vale of York and across to the Humber Estuary; an area of extensive fields vivid with the yellow of oilseed flowers or ripening corn according to the season. However, industry is by no means left behind in this area of agricultural activity, for in many places the view is dominated by the cooling towers of the power-stations at Eggborough and Drax, two of the largest in the country. Throughout the day the line is busy with a stream of coal trains that supply an annual total of some 20,000,000 tons of coal to the two plants. Much of this coal originates from Kellingley Colliery, which is situated on the left of the line a mile or so out of Knottingley. Sunk in the early 1960s, it is the largest single mine in Europe with an annual output of over 20,000,000 tons, and employs about 2,000 men. Miners from areas badly affected by pit closures in the 1960s were attracted to Kellingley and the promise of secure employment; as a result it is far from unusual to hear Scottish or Geordie accents on the streets of Knottingley.

Alongside the colliery the line crosses over the Knottingley and Goole Canal, opened by the Aire and Calder Navigation Company in 1826, and whose course we will parallel for the remainder of the journey. Although much of the canal's staple coal traffic was claimed by the railway, it remains a working waterway with oil and coal barges plying their way between the Humber ports, Castleford, and Leeds.

The next stop is at Whitley Bridge, a straggling village astride the Selby to Doncaster road. An early model Lancashire & Yorkshire Railway signal-box controls the level crossing and junction with the branch to Eggborough power-station, which diverges to the left shortly after the station. After this the line passes through a comparative rarity—a shallow cutting—and over a couple more level crossings before reaching Hensall. The station here retains a charming Victorian atmosphere with another L & Y signal-box, the original wooden waiting-room on the westbound platform, and the imposing station house on the opposite side. Though now in private occupation, its former ownership is still proudly proclaimed in stained glass on the front entrance and the present owner has recently fixed several vintage enamelled advertisement signs on the walls.

Hensall itself is a quiet farming village which lies mainly to the north of the line. The Railway Inn, adjacent to the station, serves the locally brewed Old Mill Bitter. Shortly after leaving Hensall the train passes beneath the East Coast main line and reaches the junction of the branch to Drax power-station. This branch forms part of the route of the long-defunct Hull & Barnsley Railway, a bold attempt to break the monopoly held by the North Eastern on the transport of coal between South Yorkshire and Hull Docks. The H & B never quite succeeded in its ambition and, apart from a short stretch of track which survives in the Hull suburbs, the entire route had closed by 1955. The supply of coal to Drax, however, has resulted in several miles of the line being reinstated together with a new connection on to the Knottingley-Goole line. The chimney at Drax, incidentally, is the highest in the country at 850 feet.

Beyond the junction with the Drax branch, the 'main' line is now reduced to a single track, having only the passenger service and a daily freight from Goole to York to handle; a stark comparison with its heyday as a coast express route. The first station on this section is at Snaith, an attractive small town built largely of weathered red brick. The town is centred around Market Place, adjacent to the station, at one end of which stands the squat Priory Church of St Laurence.

Beyond Snaith the line continues its course across the flat terrain, punctuated by a succession of level crossings, to the next stop at Rawcliffe. The station, standing in the shadow of the M62 which crosses the line on a high embankment, serves a fair-sized village, the majority of which is situated to the north of the railway. The oldest part of Rawcliffe stands on the bank of the River Aire, a mix of red brick and colour-washed houses around a large tree-shaded green, the centre-piece of which is the Parish Church of St James. There is some industry, however, as we soon pass a large paper-mill and then, for the final stage of the journey into Goole, run alongside the twin waterways of the Knottingley and Goole Canal and the peculiarly named Dutch River. Being very close to sea-level, the land hereabouts was prone to flooding from the River Don; however, in 1684 the Dutch engineer Cornelius Vermuyden was appointed to drain the marshland and straighten the course of the river, enclosing it between high floodbanks. It is quite noticeable that the water-level of the canal is higher than the railway.

In common with many other ports, the amount of rail traffic handled at Goole is a shadow of its former level, a fact that can be judged from the overgrown site of sidings on our left. At least the port still does some business with the railway, however; the line to the docks branches off to the right and a pair of shunters are based at the port. There is also a healthy trade in imported cars, evidenced as we pass the loading ramp shortly before joining the main line for the last few yards into Goole Station, with its typical North Eastern Railway footbridge and platform canopies. There are several places worth seeing in Britain's most inland port—Chapter 3 has the details.

## SHEFFIELD TO YORK

**by Peter Cookson**

The present-day traveller from Sheffield to York will use one of three routes: if he is using an InterCity service from the south-west to the north-east he will very likely travel via Doncaster or possibly via Leeds, but the traveller on the local Dearne Valley service, better known as the Swinton & Knottingley Joint Line, will go through Pontefract, and this is the route described here, although the service on this route is irregular and confined to six or seven trains a day.

The line from Sheffield to Rotherham is described in Chapter 7. On leaving Rotherham the line follows the Don Valley and still the landscape remains the same: Parkgate Steelworks is seen on the left near to the closed station of Rawmarsh and very soon the important Aldwarke Junction is passed, where the former LMS and LNER lines came close together and now make important connections. The observant traveller may see vestiges of a station at Kilnhurst but also a change in the industrial landscape: the dominant industry is no longer steel. Near to Kilnhurst on the right-hand side can be seen tar-distillers, glassworks and, in places, colliery headgear. We are now entering the coal-mining belt. The urban area spreading out to the left is Swinton and that to the right is Mexborough; the former has now lost its station on the Midland line but the latter retains its station on the Sheffield–Doncaster route.

Just beyond the point at which the railway crosses over the former Doncaster–Barnsley line at Mexborough is the site of the former Wath Road Junction (not now a junction) where the Swinton & Knottingley Joint Line diverged to York. It was opened in 1879 to provide a direct route from the Midland to the North Eastern system, avoiding the very congested stretch of line through Normanton. The site of the junction is only now discernible in that two of the four running lines curve away north-westwards towards Cudworth, Normanton, and Leeds, while the S & K line strikes due north over the valley of the Dearne (from which the Sheffield–Pontefract–York service takes its name).

Nowhere along the line is the coal-mining landscape seen more clearly than at the Manvers Colliery complex at Wath-on-Dearne, seen to the left of the train as it heads away from the Wath Road. In spite of the name given to the line it does not follow the Dearne Valley at all but simply crosses it. On the northern side of the river we enter another urban area: the town spreading out to the left of the line is Bolton-on-Dearne where the station is situated. There is continuous urban development here and Bolton merges directly into Goldthorpe (mainly to the right of the line) and then into Thurnscoe. It is intended that new stations should be built to serve the communities at Swinton, Goldthorpe, and Thurnscoe. The whole area around here still produces a large amount of coal, most of it destined for the Aire Valley power-stations and using the S & K line.

The traveller will notice that on leaving Bolton-on-Dearne Station the gradient increases considerably as the railway climbs out of the Dearne Valley, and beyond Thurnscoe there is the first respite from the industrial scene as the line heads due north through rolling wooded hills in the vicinity of Frickley. There is not much to be seen here because of the cuttings, but the area is pleasant and rural; Hooton Pagnell Hall and Frickley Hall are not very far distant on the right-hand side of the line but are not visible. The rural interlude is short-lived, however, and we soon cross into West Yorkshire and enter another mining valley. Just before Moorthorpe Station, Frickley Colliery is passed on the right-hand side and the town of South Elmsall is seen also on the right. The station serves the communities of Moorthorpe, South Kirkby, and South Elmsall even though there is a station serving the last named place on the Doncaster–Leeds line. This is still a coal-mining area with other large collieries in the vicinity serving mainly the Aire Valley power-stations.

At the north end of Moorthorpe Station the InterCity route to Wakefield and Leeds diverges to the left to join the main Doncaster–Leeds line at South Kirkby Junction. All this can be clearly seen as the York line climbs out of the valley on an embankment towards Royd Moor which is the highest portion of the line. Pit heaps still scar the scene but the traveller will notice attempts to landscape the spoil, though much remains to be done. The line suffers badly from subsidence here but much work has been done in recent years to rectify the problems. Subsidence, in fact, was the main reason for the transfer of the northeast-southwest trains away from the S & K line. The climb of a couple of miles out of Moorthorpe is completed in a cutting but then the line emerges into an open rural landscape and South Yorkshire is left behind.

The line, now virtually straight for a couple of miles, is carried on a high embankment across the valley of the River Went and over the river itself (which is little more than a stream) by an elegant viaduct. The large straggling village on the left is Ackworth and the small village nestling in the trees on the right is Badsworth. Both are reasonably well known: the former for its Quaker school founded in the eighteenth century and the latter for giving its name to the hunt. Both villages have pockets of great charm. Although at one time Ackworth had a station, all that remains is the old goods shed visible on the left as the railway heads into a short cutting. The line emerges on a gradual curve on to an embankment from which the southern outskirts of Pontefract can be seen on the left. Much of the southern part of the town is obscured by a cutting as the railway takes a sweeping curve to descend to the level of Baghill Station, which lies in a valley away from the town centre.

Pontefract has a long history as a garrison and market town and was a substantial town when Sheffield was merely a hamlet. It is built on a series of low hills and on one of them stand the ruins of the Norman castle, though not a great deal remains of it. It has often been referred to as the 'Key to the North' as the great fortress kept watch over the route to the north and the crossing of the River Aire. It was eventually demolished in the seventeenth century after withstanding several sieges by the Parliamentarians in the Civil War.

Although the town has to some extent been spoilt by later unsympathetic development, the centre still retains some handsome streets and buildings with the Buttercross at the centre of a wide, traffic-free market-place. Pontefract is well worth a visit and the museum contains a permanent exhibition of the history of the town, and advice can be obtained as to suitable sites for the visitor to explore. There is a variety of industry here but perhaps the best known is the confectionery industry and in particular the manufacture of Pontefract Cakes and other liquorice sweets.

Leaving Pontefract the railway continues down gradient in a wide sweep to cross the River Aire near Brotherton just beyond Ferrybridge. Ferrybridge Junction marks the end of the old Swinton & Knottingley Railway and at this point the old North Eastern Railway metals were reached by means of the branch from Knottingley. The town of Knottingley marks the eastern edge of the industrial part of West Yorkshire, and Ferrybridge, which is now part of it, was an important stop in coaching days on the Great North Road. Although there is no longer a station at Ferrybridge there is much of interest here packed into a small area. After passing under the M62 motorway on the eastern edge of Pontefract, the railway passes under the Leeds–Goole line, is joined by branches from the right and left, runs alongside the A1 trunk road, passes two large power-stations, crosses over the River Aire by a girder bridge and plunges into a short tunnel in little over a mile. The shallow tunnel at Brotherton, like many others, was built to hide the railway from view rather than as an engineering necessity.

We are now in rural North Yorkshire and the industrial belt of South and West Yorkshire is behind us as the railway makes its easy passage along the Vale of York to the City of York. A fairly sharp curve brings us to Burton Salmon, a small village in itself, but until recently an important junction where the line from Normanton and Castleford (the old York & North Midland line) joins. This junction, however, was found to be dispensable and (as at Wath Road) all that can be seen is an extra pair of tracks coming in from the left. This set of four tracks continues as far as Milford Junction where extensive sidings for the reception of coal from the new Selby coalfield are laid out, and where the branch to Selby diverges to the right towards the new-look, late twentieth-century colliery at Gascoigne Wood. After passing under the Leeds–Selby line the train reaches Sherburn-in-Elmet Station which has recently been reopened on the site of a previous station and using the same platforms. Sherburn, in recent years, has developed from a small village to a substantial dormitory town possessing some of its own industry.

A couple of miles farther on, the railway meets the main Leeds–York line at Church Fenton, where quite a large station is provided, with platforms on both sets of tracks. The rest of the journey to York (described in Chapter 2) is relatively uneventful being almost perfectly level and straight. York Station is eventually reached some 46 miles from Sheffield in about one and a quarter hours by Dearne Valley stopping train.

# 7

# SHEFFIELD AND SOUTH YORKSHIRE

## SHEFFIELD – RAILWAY CENTRE AND CITY

**by Herbert Proctor and Peter Cookson**

Sheffield is one of the great industrial cities of the Western World and, with a population of approximately 500,000, it also ranks as one of the largest in Great Britain. Its fame is world-wide and comes from its association with steel-making and, in particular, the production of quality steels for tool-making and cutlery; the phrase 'Made in Sheffield' is a hallmark of good quality and reliability. In recent years as other countries have developed their own capacity for steel-making, the city has seen a decline, so that the rail-traveller passing through sees a city of great contrasts: from miles of suburbs in tree-lined valleys in the south to a landscape of industrial dereliction in the north. As with all our industrial towns and cities, much of the past is being swept away and rebuilding is transforming their image, but for those interested in Sheffield's past, a visit to the Abbeydale Industrial Museum is a rewarding experience.

When George Stephenson built the line from Derby to Leeds in 1840, he warned the people of Sheffield that he could only get them in and out of their town by way of Rotherham, because of the need to avoid steep gradients and extensive tunnelling. In the event, the Sheffield & Rotherham Railway was carrying passengers before the North Midland Railway arrived at Rotherham, but it was not until 1870 that the line was opened from Chesterfield to Sheffield, and Sheffield came on a direct north-south route. Since then, the sheer size of the city has attracted routes until now it is something of a nodal centre for British Rail. Liverpool and Manchester to Hull and Bristol to Newcastle meet here and the Midland route from London St Pancras terminates. The station was the largest one in the sole ownership of the old Midland Railway.

Emerging from the 1905 station building, the visitor is faced with a traffic road, an acre or two of bus stands, and a hill in the background, in part obscured by modern blocks. The centre of things runs along the crest of the hill. The visitor could do worse than to turn right and then, down on the left beyond the buses, he will find a genuine fifteenth to sixteenth-century timber-framed pub, the Old Queen's Head, the only such building in the centre of Sheffield. From here it is an easy step forward to Fitzalan Square and on via a major underpass, called locally 'the Hole in the Road', to the Cathedral, raised to this rank in 1914. What old work remains is of the fifteenth and sixteenth centuries; there are fragments of old glass and modern extensions.

Forward, down Fargate, will be found the Tourist Information Office in the Town Hall complex. Details are obtainable here of Sheffield's interesting industrial museums: the recently opened Kelham Island, Abbeydale Hamlet, and Shepherd's Wheel, of Weston Park, Bishop's House (another old timber-framed house in Meersbrook Park), and art galleries. It must be admitted that most of these places are a distance from the city centre, and as in most other towns in this country, there is little local transport except the bus. However, Kelham Island Museum is a mile west of the Cathedral and Abbeydale Industrial Hamlet is within walking distance of Dore Station.

Now one for the real walker. A mile down Ecclesall Road you come to Hunter's Bar, situated in the middle of a roundabout. Here turn into Endcliffe Park and just keep on, across all roads. The path becomes less and less park-like at each crossing and you may become aware of why Sheffield grew here, where the millstone grit slides under the coal measures, for the streams were dammed to work wheels and the right stone was there. You pass the restored Shepherd's Wheel this way, and you finally emerge on the edge of the moors, and now I leave the walker to his map to go over the edge within sight of Sheffield's highest point, 1,502 feet, and down to a station on the Hope Valley line (see *Five Shires by Rail*).

## SHEFFIELD–ROTHERHAM

**by Herbert Proctor and Peter Cookson**

For 11 miles out of Sheffield, there are two roughly parallel lines and in immediately pre-BR days, the LNER route on the east, from Sheffield Victoria, carried all the Doncaster passenger traffic. The route is now of a composite nature, leaving Sheffield on Midland metals. The northern exit from Sheffield is like so many others in our large cities and towns; the line threads its way through a series of cuttings and tunnels criss-crossed at frequent intervals by city streets until it emerges on an embankment to pass through the tiny station of Attercliffe Road and cross over the River Don on its way through the northern suburbs. There is little housing to be seen and it is on this stretch of line that so much dereliction is to be found, but even here there is much activity in places; steel-mills both working and closed, scrap-yards, railway sidings, and other industrial premises follow in quick succession. The next station is Brightside, still in the heavy industrial belt and about midway between Sheffield and Rotherham. Just before Brightside Station a branch diverges to the right and runs into the large Tinsley marshalling yards and a little way after the station the branch to Barnsley via Chapeltown diverges to the left. North of the line on the left, there is a listed site on Wincobank Hill below which the line passes, with Wincobank Camp, the Roman Rig, and Iron Age earthworks, within a mile of Brightside Station. From this point a good view is obtained of the large viaduct which carries the M1 motorway over the Don Valley: in some respects the motorway acts as a physical boundary between Sheffield and Rotherham.

With no change of scenery on the next stretch of line, the railway takes a rather sharp left-hand bend and brings us into Rotherham Masborough Station where the original North Midland line is joined and seen trailing in on the right-hand side of the train. For travellers interested in railway stations it is possible to see here some of the Midland characteristics still remaining, especially in the platform awnings. Masborough Station is not very convenient for the centre of this large and important town and in May 1987 a new station opened at Rotherham Central on the old LNER (GC) route from Sheffield to Doncaster which has paralleled the Midland route to this point-and continues to do so as far as Swinton. This development should make the town more accessible for shoppers and visitors. Like its larger neighbour, Rotherham has experienced a serious decline in its heavy industry but is fighting back by encouraging new industrial enterprises to replace the old.

# ROTHERHAM

**by Herbert Proctor**

The church is the show-piece and dominates the centre. Mainly Perpendicular, it is described by Professor Pevsner as one of the largest and stateliest in Yorkshire. There is, too, a medieval Bridge Chapel – on its original bridge. Clifton Park is near the centre, with Clifton House (1782), residence of Joshua Walker, ironmaster. It is now a pleasant intimate museum with Roman pillars from Templeborough outside and some relics of the Sheffield & Rotherham Railway inside. One of the town's most noted sons was Thomas de Rotheram, Archbishop of York (1480-1500), who built his Jesus College here. There are little-known remnants of this still existing, part of a shop in the Woolworth complex.

# ROTHERHAM – DONCASTER

**by Herbert Proctor**

North of Rotherham, where the two lines come within a stone's throw of each other, BR has constructed Aldwarke Junction, a scissors-type crossing between the two lines. At the time of writing, Doncaster trains cross from the western line to the eastern line at this point, but when Rotherham Central Station comes into use, in May 1987, that will not be necessary for trains routed via that station. Trains for Leeds and York keep straight ahead at this point and pass out of the Don Valley beyond Swinton, about 2 miles on. It might be noted here that a curve may be reinstated at Swinton to enable trains to pass to the Doncaster line at Mexborough without going over Aldwarke Junction and, as a consequence, Swinton Station may be reopened. Should this come about, then local trains from Rotherham Central will use the opposite chord at Aldwarke to call at Swinton before proceeding to Mexborough.

At Swinton, the valley turns to the east and the Doncaster line turns with it. Mexborough is soon reached, where the station is a handsome stone building and

Conisbrough Castle, by the River Don *(Photo: David Thurlow)*

probably the best building in the town. This town, with its small market, has some local importance, and at one time there was a free ferry over the Don for people from Denaby village on the other side. There is now a footbridge. There is a small park with what is left of an old castle.

The line crosses the Don and reaches the station at Conisbrough, half-way between that place and the mining settlement of Denaby Main. On the north, the river Dearne comes in. In the little mining town is Conisbrough Castle, an ancient monument of national importance, in the care of the Royal Commission. Dating from about 1190 the impressive stone tower keep has a chapel in one buttress and there are substantial remains of the curtain-wall, with some solid towers. The castle owes its excellent state of preservation to the fact that it was not defensible by the time of the Civil War and consequently remained unslighted by Cromwell's forces. Do not overlook Conisbrough Church, a gem of an old building, some parts of which pre-date the castle. The castle and the area figure prominently in Sir Walter Scott's *Ivanhoe.*

On from Conisbrough and passing Cadeby Colliery on the north, the route takes on a slightly bizarre aspect. Ahead is a belt of magnesian limestone, there is a short tunnel and then a long rock cutting, and one presently perceives that here the limestone has been exploited for commercial purposes, so that the cutting conceals vast pits and excavations. Elsewhere this stone belt produces fine villages and scenes of beauty, but here the beauty has been destroyed.

Following a green sweep of the Don below, the river enters a flat landscape. There is no more of note in running through the suburbs of Doncaster, but just before entering the station, notice on the right-hand side a little church with a turret oddly sited partly on the west gable. This was built in 1858 by the Great Northern Railway, and was designed by (the later) Lord Grimthorpe.

## SHEFFIELD–WORKSOP–RETFORD

**by Herbert Proctor**

The route starts over a spur in the deep cutting immediately north of Sheffield Station. It climbs up to the old LNER route from Sheffield Victoria, with a wide view to the north of the 'East End' of Sheffield, once covered with a forest of works smoke-stacks. After passing the small island platform of Darnall, the train crosses in a cutting from the Don Valley to that of the Rother. Orgreave Colliery is passed on the left shortly before Woodhouse Station.

Beyond this outer suburban district, the line crosses the Rother Valley and over the old line of the North Midland Railway. In 1963, this line was shown on Beeching's maps as one of the densest routes for freight traffic in the country. It is once again possible to travel over part of this line on a passenger service, since some Glasgow–Nottingham trains arrive at Sheffield from Manchester at the south end of the station, and then head north and round on to this line in order to reach Chesterfield without reversal.

A rural mile or two follows past the site of Waleswood Station, and then comes Kiveton Park, a long straggling township. Until 1929 the only station was at the far end of the urban area, but in that year the LNER opened a station in the centre and named it 'Kiveton Bridge', this being a good example of the wisdom of siting stations where the population is, for this is probably now the most important station between Sheffield and Worksop. A mile farther on comes Kiveton Park Station, with the colliery adjacent, and the line then passes into Nottinghamshire amid pleasant wooded country, continuing to Worksop, centre of Bassetlaw District, and to Retford, as described in *Five Shires by Rail.*

CARLISLE
Appleby
Windermere
Oxenholme
BARROW
Garsdale
PASSENGER RAILWAYS IN YORKSHIRE
Including principal lines and selected stations in the adjoining areas.
Lines described in this book
Other lines with regular service
Lines with occasional service
Principal InterCity Stations
Other staffed stations
Unstaffed stations
Yorkshire boundary
Carnforth
Morecambe
Giggleswick
Settle
LANCASTER
Yorkshire Dales Railway
Skipton
Ilkley
Keighley & Worth Valley Railway
Clitheroe
Colne
BLACKPOOL
Burnley
BRADFORD
Blackburn
PRESTON
Accrington
Hebden Bridge
Halifax
Spen Valley Rly
Dewsbur
Todmorden
Southport
HUDDERSFIELD
Rochdale
Marsden
BOLTON
Oldham
Wigan
Penisto
MANCHESTER
Stalybridge
St Helens
LIVERPOOL
Earlestown
STOCKPORT
Warrington
North Wales

ARLINGTON
Tees side
Whitby
N
North York
Moors Railway
Northallerton
SCARBOROUGH
Pickering
Thirsk
Filey
Malton
Bridlington
Knaresborough
Driffield
HARROGATE
YORK
Beverley
EEDS
Selby
Gilberdyke
HULL
Middleton
Rly
Brough
Goole
AKEFIELD
Barton on Humber
Pontefract
Thorne
Scunthorpe
GRIMSBY &
CLEETHORPES
Barnsley
DONCASTER
Rotherham
10 miles (16 km)
Gainsborough
EFFIELD
Worksop
Retford

# 8

# HALLAM AND PENISTONE: COAL AND SUMMER WINE

## SHEFFIELD–BARNSLEY–WAKEFIELD –LEEDS

**by Steve Wiltshire**

*(The Hallam Line–Hallam is the ancient name for South Yorkshire.)*

This is a rather neglected and unglamorous part of the railway, which serves a part of the country that does not feature prominently in tourist guidebooks. Its passenger train service consists almost entirely of local DMUs, the only exceptions being the daily return HST between Barnsley and London St Pancras and a Scarborough–Sheffield train on summer Saturdays. Train speeds are generally slow due to numerous curves, steep gradients, and subsidence caused by coal-mining, which is one of the main features of this area. An unpromising introduction, maybe, and yet this line has many interesting features for the traveller to note. It passes through a great variety of scenery: industrial and residential urban areas, agricultural land and wooded hilly country–changing in character with each curve of the track.

## SHEFFIELD–BARNSLEY

The northern exit from Sheffield Station is something of a bottleneck, with trains on four routes sharing one pair of tracks. For the first 3 miles, Barnsley trains run along the main line to Rotherham and Doncaster; some of the trains call at Attercliffe and–ironically named–Brightside stations in the devastated industrial area which was once the heart of the British steel industry.

This is the easiest and flattest exit from Sheffield and is described in Chapter 7. That changes abruptly when the Barnsley line proper diverges from the main line at Wincobank, just beyond Brightside Station. It immediately starts to twist and turn and climbs steeply as it leaves the northern suburbs of Sheffield. The M1 motorway runs parallel to the railway, a short distance away; it is encountered again several times between Sheffield and Leeds.

The first stop for most trains is at Chapeltown where a new station was opened in 1982–just 200 yards south of the former station, but much better located for the town centre. This was widely condemned at the time, as an unnecessary extravagance on the part of South Yourkshire County Council. However, the criticism was soon silenced when the number of passengers at the new station grew to nearly twice the number that had used the old one. The platforms of the old station are still visible immediately to the north of the present ones.

Next comes Tankersley Tunnel–just over ¾ mile long. From this the line emerges into one of its more rural sections for about 1 mile before reaching the next station in the village of Elsecar, which also serves the larger village of Hoyland. Just a short

Yorkshire NUM Headquarters, Barnsley *(Drawing: Suzanne Myers, courtesy of Barnsley Borough Council)*

distance farther to Wombwell and then the line turns into a switchback. This can well be appreciated from the front of one of the old-style DMUs.

On a viaduct over the River Dove at Worsbrough Dale, the line crosses over the trackbed of the former Manchester-Sheffield and Wath electrified lines, now sadly closed and lifted. This was the foot of the infamous Worsbrough Bank (gradient 1 in 40) for which, in steam days, Sir Nigel Gresley built his unique and very powerful Garrett locomotive to assist freight trains up the bank. This trackbed is just one of many remnants of the former (very complicated) railway network around Barnsley.

## BARNSLEY

Barnsley Station, the only staffed station between Sheffield and Leeds or Huddersfield, is entered over one of the very few level crossings on BR in this area. On the left can be seen the market hall and the stalls of the open market. This is one of the town's most popular attractions and the trains are usually crowded with shoppers on market days (Wednesday, Friday, and Saturday and the antiques market on Tuesday).

Barnsley Station, formerly Barnsley Exchange in the days when there were two of them, now has two platforms, but prior to 1960 there was only one—the northbound one, where the station buildings are. Evidence of the town's other station can be seen outside. The ornate Court House which was converted into the station building still stands on the opposite side of the road and part of the embankment which carried the railway into the station forms the back wall of the bus station. The bus station backs on to the BR station, making a good transport interchange. Thus Barnsley is a convenient railhead for people wishing to visit places in the district which are not served directly by rail, such as the twelfth-century Monk Bretton Priory, or Worsbrough Mill Country Park with its Museum of Industrial Archaeology.

It is worth stopping a while for a look at the town. The town itself sits mostly on a slope, facing north-east, above the valley of the River Dearne. Near the top of this slope, about ¼ mile from the station up Regent Street, sits the Town Hall—imposing four-storey building capped by a 145-foot clock tower, a prominent landmark clearly visible from the railway. The building is made of white Portland stone, contradicting the darker image of the town.

Probably Barnsley's best-known building is ¼ mile north of the Town Hall on the Huddersfield Road—an ornate two-storey Victorian mansion which is headquarters for the Yorkshire Area of the National Union of Mineworkers. Among its interesting architectural features are some fine stained-glass windows depicting mining scenes.

The mention of glass is a reminder of the town's other main industry—glass-blowing—which is of sufficient importance that the town's coat of arms incorporates the figures of a miner and a glass-blower, both sharing equal prominence. Also linen-weaving was very important to the local economy during the nineteenth-century and there are still a number of clothing-manufacturers in the area. Barnsley industry and commerce is in fact much more diverse than is generally realised, and has become more so in recent years. Until April 1986 the Metropolitan County of South Yorkshire had its headquarters here, and following metropolitan county abolition some county-wide functions are still controlled from Barnsley.

Heading south from the Town Hall, it is about another ¼ mile to the main shopping area which has been redeveloped and pedestrianised to create an attractive precinct. The modern market hall is here. Many of the older buildings have been retained in conservation areas which are appropriately described in the District Council's official guide as 'a mixed bag of charms'. Anyone feeling hungry after a walk around might like to visit one of the town's restaurants to try some of the local cuisine. A notable speciality is the 'Barnsley Chop', a mutton chop weighing about 1½ lb!

## BARNSLEY—WAKEFIELD

Leaving Barnsley Station, the line divides after about ¼ mile. The left-hand route towards Penistone and Huddersfield climbs away steeply, while the right-hand one towards Wakefield drops. On leaving Barnsley it is about 150 feet above the River Dearne. When it crosses the river about 2 miles farther north it is nearly down to the same height.

Soon comes Darton Station, a pair of wooden platforms serving a straggling mining and industrial village. Darton is in South Yorkshire, but the boundary with West Yorkshire is just north of the station. This has resulted in financial support for the train service from West Yorkshire Passenger Transport Executive in addition to support from South Yorkshire PTE. Darton is, therefore, unique in being part of two adjacent PTE networks and passengers can make a through journey using only PTE tickets. Normally PTE areas stop at the last station before a boundary, leaving a bit of 'no-man's land' between them.

Soon after leaving Darton, the train is dwarfed by the huge pit-head buildings of Woolley Colliery. Several small mines have been joined up under the ground to bring all their coal to the surface here, and it is unusual to pass it now without seeing a long train of hoppers being loaded up. Woolley is a good example of the sudden contrasts which characterise this part of the country: on the right-hand side is the large pit with its inevitable spoil heaps, while on the left is pleasant rolling wooded countryside. This is a part of Bretton Country Park, run by Wakefield Metropolitan District Council, which includes a Nature Reserve area and, a feature of particular interest, the Yorkshire Sculpture Park. This can be reached by bus from Wakefield or Barnsley to the village of West Bretton, followed by a short walk, or by a longer walk from Darton Station (2 or 3 miles) along the Dearne Way, a footpath following the river, which flows down through the park.

Woolley Edge is an escarpment which forms a prominent part of the local landscape. The railway tunnels underneath it through two separate single-track tunnels, a few yards short of a mile in length. In the cutting which follows these tunnels, the effects of subsidence are particularly visible as the track has been raised considerably above the floor of the cutting on deep ballast.

Descending steeply now, Crigglestone Junction is passed. A branch line turns off here to Healey Mills on the Wakefield—Huddersfield route. This is now used only by coal trains from Woolley. We go into another cutting, where a grand viaduct looms overhead.

This is a remnant of the Midland Railway's branch line to Dewsbury—long since abandoned and much of its course now obliterated.

The line now comes out into the valley of the River Calder, crossing, in quick succession, the Calder and Hebble Navigation, then the river itself. This is the end of the steeply graded part of the route which now curves to the right and joins the main Calder Valley line from Mirfield at Horbury Junction. In the angle between the converging railways is a complex of sidings which serves the works of Procor Ltd, builders and repairers of railway wagons. An interesting selection of wagons can usually be seen here.

To the right of the line (quadruple track now) are flooded gravel workings, split in two by the M1, which are home for a sailing club and numerous water birds, also much frequented by anglers. This part of the Calder Valley, just west of Wakefield, already offers various opportunities for recreation and there are plans for a large sports and leisure complex which have aroused much opposition. Looking farther right, on the skyline, is the ruined Sandal Castle, a prominent landmark due to its commanding position overlooking the valley and the city of Wakefield.

The line enters Wakefield, passing under the long, low viaduct which carries the main Doncaster—Leeds Railway. This is generally known as the 'Ninety-nine arches'. The short curve connecting the city's two stations trails in on the left, past an abandoned dog-track, and then Kirkgate Station is reached. This station (usually pronounced like 'Kergate') is only a shadow of its former self. It was Wakefield's first railway station and once the busier of the two, with an over-all roof covering the platform area which is now mostly open to the elements. It has recently been reduced in status to an unstaffed halt—probably the largest in the country. The station buildings, which are of some architectural interest, are still occupied by BR's civil engineering department and this has prevented the station from degenerating to the derelict state of most unstaffed stations. Unfortunately due to recurrent hooliganism, the late evening train service between Wakefield and Barnsley has been suspended on Fridays and Saturdays for a number of years.

Places of interest in Wakefield are fully described in Chapter 1, but mention should be made here of the Chantry Chapel. This chapel is in the middle of the River Calder, being built on to the old road bridge, and is only a stone's throw from Kirkgate Station, and clearly visible from the train.

## WAKEFIELD—NORMANTON—LEEDS

Back on the railway, immediately east of Kirkgate Station is a triangular junction to a line which is only occasionally traversed by passenger trains. It runs up to join the main lines to Doncaster and Sheffield, and also carries freight traffic to Knottingley via Featherstone. In recent years BR have considered ways to 'rationalise' the railway network in this area. Now, however, the existing route through Westgate has been confirmed as the principal InterCity line and is being prepared for electric trains. This threw doubt on to the future of the route to Leeds via Normanton, part of which was proposed for closure, but happily has now been reprieved.

Leaving Wakefield, the River Calder is crossed again. This in an area of great interest for waterway enthusiasts. The navigable waterways were created partly by building new canals and partly by improving the existing rivers. To the left here is a junction of the two types—the river and the Aire and Calder Canal. The river meanders but the canal goes in a straight line and crosses over the top of the river on the Stanley Aqueduct, about 1 mile north of the railway and (just about) visible from it. Another interesting feature here is the Half Moon—a part of the original course of the river which was cut off by the railway, creating an isolated backwater which is a haven for wildlife and popular with anglers.

To the left of the line is a site known as 'Welbeck', an extensive area of spoil tips left behind by several coal-mines which are now closed. At present this has the appearance of a lunar landscape but it will change dramatically over the next ten or so years thanks to an imaginative reclamation scheme. This will involve using domestic refuse and colliery spoil as landfill material and will eventually make this a landscaped area with woods and grassland.

The train now slows to negotiate Goose Hill Junction. The Wakefield–Normanton route was part of the original main line from Manchester to York and the route which joins from the right was the Midland Railway's main line from London and Sheffield to Leeds and the North. Normanton Station, about ½ mile farther on, was the most important junction in Yorkshire during the early days of railways. For a time it was a refreshment stop for express trains from London to Scotland. Its strategic location gave it extensive freight yards and engine sheds. Today most of this has been swept away and the area has a forlorn appearance. Few trains of any importance pass this way now–except at week-ends, when the line comes into its own as a diversionary route of great versatility. It can be used by trains on at least half a dozen lines when their normal routes are closed for maintenance or any other reason.

Leaving Normanton, the line comes out into flat, open country. This is close to the junction between the rivers Aire and Calder. This line comes down the Calder Valley, across the M62, and curves gently to the left to go up the Aire Valley to complete its journey to Leeds. Before it does this, it passes another junction at Altofts, where the line to Castleford, Church Fenton, and York swings off to the right. The only regular passenger services on that line at present are during the summer. Most trains go straight ahead at this junction and past Altofts. Since the two pits which it once served are long since closed and most of the surrounding houses demolished, most of the village of Altofts is closer to Normanton Station than to this one which purports to serve it. As a result it is now proposed that Hallam line trains will be diverted via Castleford (involving a reversal)–probably in 1988, and Altofts Station closed.

A mile to the north of Altofts, after crossing the Aire and Calder Navigation again, comes Methley Junction where the line from Castleford comes in from the right. This could be a better site for a station than Altofts. Two miles farther on comes Woodlesford Station, and a further 6 miles alongside the Aire brings us to Leeds. The surroundings of this section are again overwhelmingly industrial, as described at the beginning of Chapter 6, but even here contrast is maintained by Temple Newsom House and Park, visible across the valley to the right.

# BARNSLEY–PENISTONE–HUDDERSFIELD

**by Richard Fieldhouse**

It is only since 1983 that the Huddersfield service has used the route from Barnsley to Penistone. The line used to have a passenger service up to 1959, when all the local stations on the route were closed and trains withdrawn. A freight service continued on the line until 1984 when the coal trains from Dodworth Colliery were stopped. Prior to 1983 the route to Penistone was direct on the main Great Central line up the Don Valley, which has now been closed and dismantled.

Leaving Barnsley, the Huddersfield train branches sharply to the left and commences a climb of 1 in 50. This is the steepest gradient on the line and it is this section to Dodworth which is often a source of trouble to trains gaining track adhesion, particularly in the autumn and winter. The line gradient eases to 1 in 67 as the train enters a steep-sided cutting where the single track commences. The cutting levels out into a wide area which is the former site of Summer Lane Station, bounded by some old industrial buildings, after which the line crosses the M1 motorway on a long, steel girder bridge. When the motorway was constructed the line was slightly diverted as well as made single track. The end of the diversion is at the former entrance to Dodworth Colliery sidings where the present line diverges sharply to the left before crossing the main A628 trunk road by a level crossing controlled by Dodworth signal-box. At this point the character of the line changes dramatically as it passes into pleasant undulating farming country with lovely views on the right towards Cawthorne and the south-facing escarpment of High Hoyland. For the walker it is well worth leaving the train at Silkstone Common. This is a new station opened in 1984, after closure of the previous station on the site in 1959.

The lines continues to climb and passes the site of West Silkstone Junction which used to be a very busy and bustling place, as banking locomotives (both steam and electric) were detached at this junction after pushing heavy freight trains up the Worsbrough Incline. Nothing now remains at this junction other than one single track. Beyond this point the line enters Oxspring Tunnel and then crosses the Don River Valley by the stone-arched Oxspring Viaduct. The traveller is now about to join the route of the old main line from Sheffield and there is evidence of a vast area of open land which was once the site of a large number of railway sidings. This area is on the outskirts of Penistone, and after passing the elevated signal-box on the left the line swings sharply to the right and enters the curved platforms of the Huddersfield line. Penistone is the first place after leaving Barnsley where there is a passing loop.

Penistone is a small industrial town in a rural area. It is the centre for many smaller villages and has a large market on a Thursday. There are many walks possible and Langsett Moors and Dunford Bridge are within reach. The line leaves Penistone on a sharp reverse curve and enters single track on the twenty-nine-arch stone viaduct which crosses the Don River Valley again. This viaduct has a most extraordinary accident associated with it in 1916 when two arches and an engine collapsed into the river. Miraculously the engine crew jumped clear, but the engine had to cut up on site. The country surrounding the line is now much bleaker, with more small hill farms. Views are soon lost as the train enters Wellhouse Tunnel. After the tunnel, only fleeting views are now possible as the line passes through shallow cuttings as it follows the best contour route through the Pennine uplands. The railway embankments from here to Stocksmoor are a wonderful sight in August and September with purple heather. Finally the line breaks through a cutting on to a short embankment and crosses the steep-sided Dearne Valley by a high stone-arched viaduct into Denby Dale Station. There is a good view of the village from the viaduct to the right of the one of the remaining local textile mills on the left.

Denby Dale is famous for its giant meat and potato pies, the last of which was baked in 1964. Another is planned in 1988. A museum of the 1964 pie relics and those of earlier years back to 1846 are on show at the Pie Hall. The present viaduct was constructed in 1880 replacing an earlier timber structure that was considered unsafe. The contractors, Naylor's, who built the stone viaduct remained in Denby Dale and established a clay-pipe works. They are still a major employer in the area. The pipe works is adjacent to the station and used to have private siding connections.

Leaving Denby Dale the train enters a long cutting that leads to Cumberworth Tunnel. This tunnel takes the line from the Dearne Valley to the upper reaches of the Fenay Beck Valley above Kirkburton. Clayton West Junction signal-box is reached shortly, where the line becomes double track for the remainder of the route to Huddersfield. Another branch line joined here from Clayton West and was closed in 1983 and the track lifted in 1986. From this point there are some good views across the upper valley to the Emley Moor ITV transmitter mast. Shepley village can be seen on the left as the train enters the station which has staggered platforms. Shepley was well known for its tailors and also its stone quarries, one of which is still in operation. Stone used to be a major source of traffic from Shepley goods yard, and during the Second World War Shepley was the railhead for munitions, much of which were stored along the roadsides in the Sovereign area.

Some lovely views can be seen from the train down the Fenay Beck Valley to Thunderbridge and beyond towards Kirkburton. Just before Stocksmoor Station the line crosses a high embankment across a wooded tributary valley to Fulstone. Stocksmoor is off the main roads and poorly served by bus, but is a very good centre for commence a walk over the hills into *Summer Wine* country which is very close. Leaving Stocksmoor Station the line enters a deep cutting and then penetrates the hillside by means of Thurstonland Tunnel to enter the Holme Valley at a high level above Brockholes village, before reaching Brockholes Station. This was the junction of a branch line to Holmfirth which joined from the left, but new house-building now obscures much of the line which closed to passengers in 1959 and was lifted in 1966. Holmfirth is a 3-mile walk from the station, but buses are more easily accessible from Honley Station.

From Brockholes Station the line now falls on a steady 1 in 100 gradient, passing through cuttings as well as crossing a very high embankment, before entering Honley Station. From this point some splendid views of the Pennine Hills can be obtained, with Meltham Cop being a prominent shape, and *Summer Wine* scenes abound. Honley Village can also be seen on the opposite side of the valley to the station. Honley is also a good centre for commencing a walk, particularly to the Castle Hill area, the site of a Roman fort which dominates Huddersfield. A memorial tower, built in 1897 on the hill, identifies the site.

Leaving Honley Station the line runs through the short Honley Tunnel under a road and then through a cutting before reaching Robin Hood Tunnel. This tunnel takes the line through a difficult part of the Holme Valley and follows the straightest route. The line continues through a rock-lined cutting and passes the site of Berry Brow Station, closed in 1966. This station had some famous sculptures carved on the rock sides of the cutting which have now been removed and preserved at York. Shortly after the former station the train breaks out of the cutting and crosses the valley and River Holme by the magnificent Lockwood Viaduct, when some splendid views can be obtained.

The other end of the viaduct used to be the junction of the branch line to Meltham which was closed to passengers in 1949. The trackbed can be seen on the left forming a shelf above the valley floor, and now serves as a footpath. From this point industrial development is evident, some of the factory buildings being of recent construction and located on the site of extensive former railway sidings before Lockwood Station is reached. Lockwood is a suburb of Huddersfield and the station mainly serves the needs of workers to the surrounding industry.

The train, leaving Lockwood Station, immediately enters Lockwood Tunnel which takes the line into the Colne Valley which it shortly crosses by yet another viaduct. Paddock Viaduct is a combination of stone arches and lattice girders supported on stone piers for the centre section. A 'Lowry scene' of the industry of Huddersfield can be seen from both sides of the train, though there are now fewer mill chimneys and sadly a number of derelict areas where there was once a mill.

Shortly Springwood Junction is reached where the main Manchester to Huddersfield line is joined. This can be seen emerging from Gledholt Tunnels on the left, and immediately both lines enter Springwood Tunnel which ends at the entrance to Huddersfield Station. The Penistone branch leads to the centre island platform and all branch trains terminate here. Before 1960 there was a through service to Halifax and Bradford and a strong case exists for reopening this route. Indeed this is the number one candidate for reopening in Yorkshire.

Although a rather plain interior, the exterior of Huddersfield Station is one of the grandest. The station frontage is 416 feet long and comprises eight free-standing sandstone Corinthian columns 68 feet under a pediment and connected by Corinthian colonnades of eight columns to smaller buildings at the outer ends, each fronted by four columns. These buildings formerly housed the booking offices and waiting-rooms of the Lancashire & Yorkshire Railway and the London & North Western Railway companies. The L & Y R office was at the Penistone end of the station and the company coat of arms is carved in stone and surmounts the columns. Likewise the LNWR was at the Leeds end of the station and the station was operated jointly up to 1922. The centre section of the station was formerly a hotel, but is now the main booking hall. In 1968 Huddersfield Corporation purchased the whole frontage and this is now a Grade 1 listed structure. Recently the main shed roof was replaced and the station frontage roof is being replaced by Kirklees Council and restoration work of upper stonework carried out. Little of the former station frontage completed in 1852 has changed.

For the traveller from Barnsley to Huddersfield, the line is a scenic delight and an engineering marvel as it crosses the grain of the Pennines linking communities not connected by main roads. The line was under threat of closure, but the TUCC has presented a report stating that considerable hardship would result if closure took place especially for small communities such as Stocksmoor, and happily West Yorkshire P.T.A. has now agreed to resume support.

# HUDDERSFIELD

**by Richard Fieldhouse**

Having admired the splendid station frontage, turn to view the fine buildings which surround St George's Square. These were constructed when the railway and station were built, replacing some rather squalid housing. Most of the town development took place during the eighteenth and nineteenth centuries and was accelerated by the opening of the canal and later by the railway. The textile industry developed and was later followed by the engineering industry when the mills were mechanised. Mechanisation was not an easy process as the Luddite movement was strong within the town and surrounding districts. This strength of independence is a characteristic of the town and perhaps also explains the strong growth of the Nonconformist churches.

Huddersfield has one of the best textile markets in the North and this is held every Monday on a site close to the station. Textile mill shops are a speciality in the area and the worsted cloth is the best in the industry. The main shopping area is mostly predestrianised and can be found by turning right along John William Street which adjoins the square. Most of the shops are beyond the first intersection which is Kirkgate/Westgate, one of the oldest streets in the town. The parish church is in Kirkgate and the recently restored Byram Shopping Arcade in Westgate is worth exploring for the small specialist shop or restaurant. Most of the main shops are now situated between Market Street and Cross Church Street which form a box area extending to the ring road. Within this area can be found the enclosed market and the Town Hall and Concert Hall, the location for the many Choral Society performances.

There is a Tourist Information Office in the High Street/Albion Street building adjacent to the Civic Centre and the New Street shopping precinct. There are many local guidebooks, including one on some historic building trails round the town. One of the trails includes the station and buildings round St George's Square. For those interested in history, the Tolson Memorial Museum is a must. It is situated 2 miles from the town centre but can be easily reached by any bus on the Wakefield Road, the busiest road from the town. The museum contains many interesting artefacts about Huddersfield, its industry, its people, and its transport.

# 9

# ACROSS THE PENNINES

## LEEDS–HUDDERSFIELD–MARSDEN–MANCHESTER

**by Alan Haigh**

Trains on this route leave Leeds through the industrial suburb of Holbeck, and passengers need to look very closely to see signs of the old Holbeck Station which once provided interchange between the two central stations in Leeds. Diverging from the Bradford and Wakefield lines and passing under the latter, the line climbs at gradients of about 1 in 70 all the way to Morley Tunnel. Before reaching Morley it crosses over the Leeds ring road at Farnley and at this point the short freight spur to the Dunlop and Ranken Steel Company diverges on the right at Farnley Junction. Here in steam days a locomotive depot was located together with a flyover junction for the Leeds 'new' line which opened in 1899 and provided a shorter route to Huddersfield which survived until 1965.

Three miles from Leeds the line crosses over Elland Road at right angles. Here Churwell Station was located until its closure in 1939. Looking at the steepness of Elland Road it is difficult to believe that tramcars once used this road, in fact it was the scene of a major disaster in 1923 when a tramcar from Morley ran out of control and overturned at the bottom of Churwell Hill, not far from the station, with the loss of seven lives.

Today the first station on the line is at Morley, situated at the mouth of the tunnel and still trying to recover from its industrial past. Passengers visiting the town have a steep uphill ½ mile walk to reach the centre, but the town boasts two markets and an impressive Town Hall identical to that at Bolton in Lancashire. On the hillside directly to the south of Morley Station is the site of the old Morley Main Colliery which suffered a major tragedy in 1872 when an explosion resulted in thirty-four miners losing their lives. Today it is hard to imagine that this locality was once a major colliery with a mass of railway sidings.

The train plunges into Morley Tunnel, nearly 2 miles long and opened with the line in 1848 by the Leeds, Dewsbury & Manchester Railway, later to be taken over by the London & North Western Railway. The line surfaces at Batley which is the next station. Walkers can gain access here to the Leeds Country Way footpath which runs along the border of Morley and Batley. On the right, just before entering Batley Station the remains can be seen of a short branch line which ran to Birstall 2 miles away. This small town was the birthplace of Joseph Priestley who discovered oxygen and a statue of him can be seen in Birstall Market Place.

As the train leaves Batley the grandstand of the Mount Pleasant Ground of Batley Rugby League Club can be seen on the hillside on the right. The 1½ miles between Batley and Dewsbury is the heart of the heavy woollen district and the train runs along the valley with textile mills still dominating it. This area in particular specialises in woollen 'shoddy', that is the recovery of wool from old rags, in true Yorkshire tradition. Both local and Trans-Pennine express trains stop at Dewsbury, which apart

The imposing exterior of Huddersfield Station *(Photo: David Thurlow)*

from its mills is also famous for its extensive market. Next station is Ravensthorpe, not as well used as it used to be since the closure of the adjacent Thornhill power-station, now being demolished.

Directly after leaving Ravensthorpe Station the line from Wakefield joins on the left. This line, which carries a train service between Wakefield and Huddersfield, has no remaining stations open on the section between Wakefield Kirkgate (where the trains reverse) and Mirfield, although reopenings of Thornhill and Horbury Bridge have been suggested. For those interested in riding on this line, its principal items of interest are that it follows the course of the River Calder, running through the once-extensive Healey Mills marshalling yard, and passes the wagon works of Charles Roberts (now Procor) at Horbury Junction. The hourly shuttle service is designed to connect with London trains at Wakefield Westgate and does not always make good connections at Huddersfield or Wakefield Kirkgate.

Between Ravensthorpe and Mirfield the line has recently been reduced from four to three tracks. Mirfield Station gives access to some interesting walks over country or by the river, and a water-bus operates on the Calder & Hebble Canal between

Mirfield and Brighouse in the summer months. After leaving Mirfield the Huddersfield line diverges from the Calder Valley line by leaving it on the right and diving under it. Next stop is Deighton, a new station opened by West Yorkshire PTE in 1982. The station is near to two chemical works and housing, but some passengers use it for reaching Huddersfield Town Football Club. The original Deighton Station, closed in 1930, was on the Kirkburton branch, and a nearby viaduct can still be seen as one of the remains of this line.

After Deighton it is but a short run to Huddersfield, main town of the Kirklees District and most important station on this Trans-Pennine route. The town has an attractive shopping centre and fine buildings, described in Chapter 8. In particular there is the classic exterior of Huddersfield Station. A change of train can be made here on to the Denby Dale line to Sheffield. Immediately after leaving Huddersfield Station the train enters the short Springwood Tunnel to surface at Springwood Junction. Here the Sheffield route diverges on the left and Paddock Viaduct can be seen as it crosses the valley.

The train now begins the climb over the Pennines, passing through the Huddersfield suburbs of Golcar and Milnsbridge which had stations until 1968 but few remains of them can be seen today, although reopening of Milnsbridge has been considered. Farther up the Colne Valley the train stops at Slaithwaite, a station also closed in 1968 but rebuilt and reopened in 1982 by West Yorkshire PTE. The route here was once four track but today it is only double track. Slaithwaite is a good stopping-off point for walking in the Colne Valley and Scammonden Dam can be reached from the station.

Three miles up the valley we come to the sleepy but very attractive Pennine town of Marsden, where some trains terminate before returning to Leeds. For those seeking peace and relaxation there is much of interest to be found here. A short walk from the station is the tranquil spot of Marsden Moor, a property owned by the National Trust. To reach this the walker should continue from the station parallel to the railway on its right-hand side, past the mouth of the Standedge Tunnel until the path eventually peters out on Marsden Moor. By continuing over the moors access to the Pennine Way can be reached, but walkers need to have a map and be suitably equipped. Other attractions at Marsden are the Tunnel End Canal and Countryside Centre, and walks along the towpath of the Huddersfield Narrow Canal which runs by the side of the railway and is complete with picnic spots.

Through trains leaving Marsden run into the 3-mile-long Standedge Tunnel. At the other end is Greater Manchester, although the Saddleworth area including Greenfield Station was part of Yorkshire until 1974. The line emerges in Diggle, which also lost its station in 1968, and continues down the attractive, though quite thickly populated, Tame Valley, which gives its name to the Metropolitan District of Tameside. It is now downhill into Manchester with the route passing the cotton towns of Stalybridge and Ashton-under-Lyne. Two local stations, Greenfield and Mossley, are passed; only the very infrequent (every three or four hours) stopping trains call at these, but the next station, Stalybridge, is also served by Trans-Pennine trains, as it is the junction for the shuttle service to Stockport, where trains to the south form Manchester Picaddilly may be joined. After Stalybridge the main line curves off right to pass Ashton-under-Lyne Station – well placed for that town, the heart of Tameside, but again only served by the few stopping trains. From here the remaining route into Manchester Victoria passes through a fairly desolate piece of urban landscape with only two stations, Park and Miles Platting, close together at the Manchester end, and served in peak hours only. At Miles Platting the route from Leeds and Bradford via Halifax and Rochdale rejoins the Huddersfield route to share the last mile or so of steeply graded track down to the cavernous expanse of Manchester Victoria Station. This part of the line is fully described in *Lancashire and Cumbria by Rail.*

# 10

# BRADFORD AND CALDERDALE

## LEEDS–BRADFORD–HALIFAX–ROCHDALE AND BURNLEY

**by Stephen Waring**

The Caldervale line of West Yorkshire's Metrotrain network leaves Leeds by way of Whitehall and Holbeck junctions where routes to the Dales, London, the Midlands, and Huddersfield also part company. There is a steep climb past Armley Gaol (north of the line), through cuttings and then out into the open before Bramley, and on through the Stanningley area to New Pudsey.

Bramley's unstaffed halt was built for West Yorkshire County Council in 1984. It serves a densely populated area about 4 miles from the centre of Leeds. New Pudsey opened in 1967, the year when Leeds Central Station was shut and its trains transferred to the rebuilt City Station. Rather distant from Pudsey Town, New Pudsey should perhaps have been 'Leeds and Bradford Parkway', because it has a big car park and is conveniently placed on the modern road network so that people can 'park and ride' or 'kiss and ride' without having to put up with city traffic. Originally New Pudsey had regular expresses to London starting from Bradford. Now the usual advice is 'Change at Leeds'.

The railway continues its climb through Hillfoot Tunnel and reaches a summit close to Laisterdyke, nearly at Bradford. Remains of Laisterdyke Station, in a deep cutting, are hard to discern because the track has been realigned. Trains used to branch off here and take a direct route to Halifax via Bowling avoiding Bradford. Now all services descend steeply through tunnels, round a tight curve where St Dunstan's Station used to be, and past Mill Lane signal-box to Bradford Interchange.

## BRADFORD

The city of Bradford is rather a hilly place to wander around. But it has good shops and much else besides. The old parish church has been continually altered and extended over 700 years and it became the Cathedral in 1919. St George's Hall is a venue for live music, wrestling, and other events, while popular theatre is catered for by the Alhambra, wonderfully refurbished in a post-modern Classical style. Both the Alhambra and the St George's Hall have classy bars and eating facilities that make good lunchtime rendezvous.

The National Museum of Photography, Film, and Television opens from 11 a.m. till 6 p.m. (but not on Mondays) and is probably the best museum in Yorkshire. Its spectacular wider-than-wide screen IMAX cimema is worth queueing for.

Bradford still has two railway stations. The Interchange opened in 1973, replacing the grander Exchange now reduced to a disorganised car park behind the Victoria

Hotel. Bradford Interchange was one of the last big-scale local transport projects before present-day municipal frugality replaced the enthusiasm and civic pride of an earlier age. Stairs from the railway platforms and travel centre lead to the main concourse where there are shops and escalator links to the covered bus terminal.

## A WALK ACROSS BRADFORD

Leaving the Interchange on foot, continue down Bridge Street staying on the left-hand side. The Victoria Hotel and St George's Hall are across the road. At the traffic lights cross wide Hall Ings and enter Norfolk Gardens in front to the splendid City Hall. For the Photographic Museum, turn left along Norfolk Gardens, cross Channing Way, and follow the signs via a subway. Next door to the museum is the high-rise Public Library, and just down the road the unmistakable Alhambra. There is a Tourist Information Centre in the City Hall building.

For Bradford's other railway station, Forster Square, keep straight on from the Hall Ings traffic lights, cross the road by the City Hall, and turn right into Market Street. The main shops are all around here, but mainly extend upwards to the left. The far end of Market Street forms a T-junction with Cheapside. Forster Square Station is visible across the road, though the builders of a horrendous office block attempted to hide it. With time to spare at this point, turn sharp left off Cheapside and wander a few yards up Kirkgate to the Shoulder of Mutton Inn, where lunchtime food and Samuel Smith's beers are purveyed. They that hunger and thirst only after righteousness may prefer to seek out the Cathedral (Church of England) whose stocky tower can be seen overlooking the General Accident office. Turn right from Market Street into Cheapside, cross Forster Square proper at the end (the subways are helpful) and enter Church Bank. Bradford should finally be noted for the excellence of some of its curry houses.

For the less energetic, mention should be made of Bradford's Explorer Bus – a unique service which runs hourly on Wednesdays and Saturdays during the summer holiday period, linking the various Bradford museums and art galleries to the Interchange Station. The museums are all free of charge, and an 80p bus ticket is valid for unlimited use all day.

## TUNNELS TO HALIFAX

Mill Lane Junction is the bifurcation of the Bradford – Leeds and Bradford – Halifax lines. The Great Northern Railway from Leeds came 'up and over' with stiff gradients. After the initial climb to Bowling Junction – like the descent from Laisterdyke at a slope of about 1 in 50 – the Lancashire & Yorkshire's West Riding Union line on to Halifax found a flatter course, mainly by using more tunnels. At Low Moor Station, after the first tunnel, portions of trains from Leeds (via Bowling) and Bradford were coupled for Halifax and beyond. At Low Moor in 1986 much redundant railway land waits for a new use. Plans for a transport museum here, with electric traction down the old Spen Valley trackbed towards Cleckheaton, may yet bear fruit.

In all from Bradford six tunnels penetrate the hills before the railway emerges at Halifax Station, in the Hebble Valley next to Mackintosh's sweet factory. Last tunnel of the six is Beacon Hill Tunnel, and the beacon far above was part of the chain that stood ready to signal from Land's End to John o' Groat's the approach of the Spanish Armada! Over the hill is the West Yorkshire Folk Museum at Shibden Hall, twenty minutes' walk from the station.

Halifax is famous for toffees, textiles, machine tools, and Rugby League, though

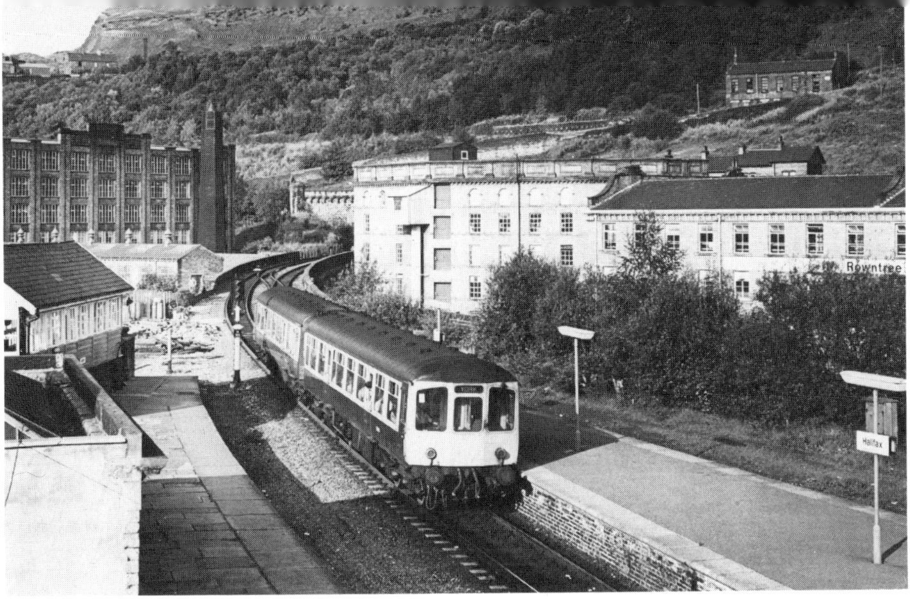


A Caldervale DMU leaves Halifax Station and enters Beacon Hill Tunnel, bound for Bradford
*(Photo: David Thurlow)*

manufacturing industry shrank distressingly during the late 1970s and early 1980s. Two minutes from the station, is the eighteenth-century Piece Hall, once an exchange for 'pieces' of cloth, later a wholesale fruit and vegetable market, now superbly restored as a centre for arty-crafty shops, galleries, Friday and Saturday open market, and numerous al fresco summer events. Next door the Calderdale Industrial Museum in a former engineering works has machines and displays that show the area's industrial history in action.

The 1891 Halifax Borough Market is the best for miles around, while the Town Hall, seat of local government for the Calderdale District, is a fine Victorian edifice designed by Charles Barry, who had a hand in the Houses of Parliament. The fifteenth & sixteenth-century Parish Church of St John the Baptist, visible from the railway station, might perhaps have merited cathedral status but for the apparent pre-eminence of Wakefield and Bradford. George Gilbert Scott of St Pancras Station fame did some refurbishing of Halifax Parish Church in 1877, having built the town's All Souls Church twenty years earlier. All Souls was itself being restored in 1986. It is some way from the station but has a spectacular location that can be appreciated from the town centre by looking north along Market Street.

A disused goods shed to the south of Halifax Station houses the national Horses at Work Museum which started up in 1986. Horse-drawn trams may eventually operate through a Heritage Centre near to the station. Halifax is looking to its past, its Victorian and pre-Victorian so-called 'inheritance', to attract visitors and some new prosperity. But the past was rarely a good time for the mass of people. Under the local Gibbet Law, finally abolished in 1650, people were beheaded for stealing goods worth 13d. or more. The Gibbet has been restored too – though not to working order. "From Hell, Hull and Halifax, Lord deliver us!"

We leave by train past Dryclough Junction where the Salterhebble Bank splits off and descends towards Greetland and a possible but unexploited route for direct trains to Sheffield. Yet another tunnel, at Bank House, curving westwards, takes the Caldervale line into the Calder Valley proper, and the original Lancashire & Yorkshire main line is joined at Milnor Royd Junction. Before the junction the River Calder is crossed by Copley Viaduct, and another Halifax eccentricity can be seen north of the line. Wainhouse Tower, technically a tall chimney built in the 1870s by dyeworks-owner J. E. Wainhouse, is evidently something of a folly. It has a taxing spiral staircase that can usually be climbed by the healthy on Spring and August Bank Holidays to reach an ornamental balcony giving an all-round view over Halifax and Sowerby Bridge.

## THE UPPER CALDER VALLEY

Sowerby Bridge and Mytholmroyd stations are now 'Paytrain'-type halts, and some of the semi-fast Preston trains do not call. Sowerby Bridge has a lively open market, plenty of industrial archaeology, and two canals. The Calder and Hebble Canal Navigation ends at the basin here, and used to be linked to the now-disused Rochdale Canal so that there was a Trans-Pennine waterway from Manchester to Castleford. Now a road blocks that link. But farther up the valley work proceeds to make the Rochdale navigable once again and boats are afloat between Hebden Bridge and Todmorden. Meanwhile, you can walk the towpath without interruption—a gentle form of exercise.

From Sowerby Bridge to Mytholmroyd, the Calder Valley is wide and the L & Y main line's curvature easy. The old station at Mytholmroyd perches above a narrow road close to the distinctive Shoulder of Mutton Inn. The station has suffered misuse since it became unstaffed, and there are plans to replace it with a simpler structure a few yards down the line. Walkley's clogg factory and mill shop stands half-way along the main road to Hebden Bridge—a nicer way to get there is to walk along the restored canal bank. The mill has eating facilities.

Hebden Bridge, 'The Pennine Centre', is picturesque and trendy. Set in the confluence of the Hebden, Colden, and Calder valleys, the small town is crowded in by steep hillsides and makes one of the most spectacular urban-rural landscapes in England. Round here are real hills, worth climbing for the views. Easier rambles also lead to pleasant scenes along the canal towpath or through the woodland of Hardcastle Craggs and Crimsworth Dean. On Wednesdays and Saturdays No. 500 bus runs between Hebden Bridge Station and Keighley via Oxenhope and Haworth.

Pennine landscape closes in as railway follows river past Hebden Bridge. The views here are best in early autumn evenings when colours are changing and sunshine still brightens the highlights. But come in winter too! Look out south of the line and spot a pointed monument high above. The monument is Stoodley Pike, and it was originally built in 1815 to commemorate the peace after the Battle of Waterloo. In 1854, Stoodley Pike fell down, a few days before the declaration of war between Victoria's Britain and the Tsar, to be rebuilt twelve years later in celebration of another peace. Today the 112-foot construction still towers high on the edge of Langfield Moor, a landmark for walkers on the Pennine Way and a magnet to attract townspeople outwards and upwards on bright summer afternoons. A good half-day ramble starts from Hebden Bridge Railway Station, passes Stoodley Pike, and ends in Todmorden.

From Stoodley Pike look down upon the Calder Valley uplands pierced by wooded tributary vales. The town of Todmorden rests in a kind of bowl and all along from there to Hebden Bridge the River Calder has seemingly worn itself a ditch, usually deep and always narrow. In the constricted bottom of the ditch people built their transport routes. The 'new' turnpike road from Halifax to Burnley is now the crowded A646. The Rochdale Canal was closed for years but is now being restored for leisure. And the Lancashire & Yorkshire Railway that had the easiest but not the most direct route from Manchester to Leeds is still possibly the most modern way of travelling through the Upper Calder Valley.

# THROUGH THE PENNINES

From Stoodley Pike you can see where the railway crosses Todmorden town on a viaduct of sandstone, and with a keener eye spot where the routes from Yorkshire diverge at Hall Royd Junction for Rochdale and Burnley. The stopping service for Manchester stays with the main line curving gently over the town. Todmorden is the last station in West Yorkshire but the first in British Rail's London Midland Region. Todmorden seems to have a split personality – not Yorkshire, not Lancashire. Part of the present town area was in the ancient parish of Halifax. Recently rule from Halifax as part of Calderdale District receives a less than warm welcome and 'Tod' looks economically and culturally towards Manchester. The postal address in 'TODMORDEN, Lancashire'.

Tourism has had less effect here than in Hebden. But there is the same good walking country, a notable Town Hall building, and a good park at Centre Vale. Undistracted, the railway holds steady its 1 in 180 climb more or less from Hebden Bridge through Todmorden, over Gauxholme Viaduct and through Walsden village to the northern portal of Summit Tunnel, appropriately named. In 1984/85 the tunnel survived what seemed to be a devastating fire that sent flames violently skywards out of the air shafts. Repairs were carried out, and tribute paid to the people that built the tunnel and George Stephenson its engineer.

Today trains pass beneath the Pennine Hills as if nothing had happened and reappear about a mile short of Littleborough Station. The landscape is more open now, and the route straightish, south to Rochdale and Manchester Victoria Station. A mile beyond Littleborough is Smithy Bridge, a new halt built at the behest of Greater Manchester County Council. At Rochdale a loop line from Oldham trails in before the sensibly modernised station is reached. The five-minute walk to the town centre is worth while. In 1844 the Rochdale Pioneers launched a great radical movement by starting a Co-operative Society, in Toad Lane. Now Toad Lane is cut in two by a new road, but a museum commemorates its place in social history. One of Rochdale's main shopping streets is called Yorkshire Street.

# THE TWO CALDERS

'Calder' is common among British place-names. At Summit village by the railway tunnel's southern portal there is a housing estate called 'Calderbrook', though the 'brook' here becomes not the River Calder but the 'Roch' that gives its name to Rochdale. Seven miles north of Calderbrook, the rocks of Thieveley Scout overlook the Cliviger Gorge and in this region two streams assemble themselves and set off in opposite directions, one east, one west – and both call themselves the River Calder.

Trains from Leeds follow the Yorkshire Calder from Sowerby Bridge to Hall Royd. Here, the 'Roses Link' service for Preston and Blackpool leaves the main line to miss Todmorden but stay with the principal valley. Gradients are harder now, curves sharper, and progress slower as the train passes the villages of Lydgate, Cornholme, and Portsmouth. Look out for dignified sandstone mills, spectacularly located. After Portsmouth level crossing the line enters Lancashire and reaches its summit at Copy Pit in the northern shadow of Thieveley. Water trickling or gushing off the rocks or down narrow cloughs here must be a seed stream of one Calder or the other.

The Lancashire Calder runs down the Cliviger Gorge past Townley Hall, then through Burnley to merge with the Ribble at a place called Whalley. Railway follows river more or less to Burnley and comes out at Gannow Junction to be joined by a single-track branch from Colne. Before the junction, Burnley Manchester Road Station reopened in October 1986 giving a convenient new stop on the route to Yorkshire. The 'Roses Link' trains started as an experiment in 1984 and early success suggests the link will be kept. Admirers of canal-engineering will want to stop at Burnley to see the straight level mile of the Leeds and Liverpool which has an aqueduct over the Calder. The Lancashire sections of these lines are fully described in *Lancashire and Cumbria by Rail*. The Copy Pit line is one of the nicest ways to enter Yorkshire by train.

# WEST YORKSHIRE TRANSPORT MUSEUM AND SPEN VALLEY RAILWAY

**by John Moore and Nigel Cross**

The West Yorkshire Transport Museum was founded by the former West Yorkshire County Council in 1983 with the aim of establishing a comprehensive transport preservation centre of potentially national statue. The project is divided into three main elements—a canal-oriented site in the Dewsbury area, a road-transport complex at Low Moor, and the interconnecting Spen Valley Railway. A site at Heckmondwike, also on the railway, is intended to serve as a secondary centre for road-transport exhibits, possibly also providing a home for the railway vehicles. The trams would be based at Low Moor with restored buses and trolleybuses. Railway stock includes a Class 506 emu from the Manchester—Glossop line, the ex-Aberdeen-Ballater battery emu, and five electric locomotives. The railway stock is not at present on view to the public except for a 600-volt dc Bo-Bo shunter from Kearsley power-station near Bolton.

The railway line down the Spen Valley was opened in 1848 by the Manchester & Leeds Railway Company (which became the Lancashire & Yorkshire Railway Company). The line ran from the main line at Mirfield, through Heckmondwike, Liversedge, Cleckheaton, and Low Moor to Bradford.

The line was always busy, particularly on the freight side. And it was not just with through freight to and from Bradford. Because of their industrial nature Cleckheaton and Heckmondwike dealt with large amounts of rail-borne traffic. This situation remained until the run-down of the railways in the 1960s. All that now remains of the once-vast railway emporium known as 'Low Moor', with its goods yards, engine sheds, and station buildings are Two West signal-box and a now-single-track junction, with track running down to the Spen Valley. The passenger service closed on 12 June 1965. Freight, in the form of Healey Mills—Bradford, lingered on until 1981.

The Low Moor site, and the line down the Spen Valley as far as Heckmondwike, has been earmarked as the main site for the proposed West Yorkshire Transport Museum. This controversial but imaginative scheme proposes to turn the Low Moor site into a museum complex, based round an Edwardian street scene. The museum is to feature buses, trolleybuses, and double-decker trams. As an integral part of the plan, the 5-mile-long Spen Valley Railway between Low Moor and Heckmondwike would be electrified at 600 volts dc using the overhead system. Trams from Blackpool, Rotterdam, Budapest, and Brussels have already been obtained, and some of these, together with motorbuses, trolleybuses, commercial vehicles, and other exhibits are on display in the museum's Ludlam Street depot and workshop near the centre of Bradford.

The Ludlam Street depot is five minutes' walk from the Interchange (just off the Manchester Road), and is open to the public on the first Sunday afternoon in each month and at other times by arrangement with the staff. Telephone Bradford (0274) 736006.

# 11
# AIREDALE AND WHARFEDALE

## LEEDS–KEIGHLEY–SKIPTON

**by Colin Speakman**

If there is a single valley which represents all that is typical of Yorkshire then it is Airedale – a river valley which starts life at the bottom of Malham Cove high in the limestone Dales and finishes up as a major industrial river and commercial waterway east of Leeds. It was the River Aire which created the city of Leeds – the highest navigable point where merchants could bring their boats to negotiate with the West Riding weavers and 'piece men' on Leeds Bridge. As the Industrial Revolution got under way, local entrepreneurs in the 1770s built that pioneering Trans-Pennine Canal all the way from Leeds Bridge to Skipton and Gargrave, finally reaching Liverpool some forty-six years later, the economic crisis caused by the Napoleonic Wars having delayed completion for two generations. If you follow the Leeds–Liverpool Canal today – which you largely do by train along the Aire Valley line – you will see evidence all round about of the immense impact of the canal on the valley, with signs of early industry, in particular the vast canal-side mills that brought the textile industry to life.

The Airedale line between Leeds, Keighley, and Skipton has an hourly train service, strengthened in the morning and evening peak and on Saturdays from May 1987, but irregular on Sundays. Several services run through to Lancaster and Morecambe. The Leeds–Carlisle trains are mostly hauled by diesel locomotives and are formed from comfortable, if ageing, corridor stock. Pacers and Sprinters are promised for these services in the not too distant future.

Almost as soon as you leave Leeds Station on the Airedale line you are into history, the line following the rail and canal corridor between Leeds and Kirkstall Abbey which now forms part of the Museum of Leeds Trail from the city centre – a quite remarkable corridor of Industrial Revolution architecture. Within 2 miles of the station, you are into the Kirkstall Valley, the River Aire on the right, the Leeds–Liverpool Canal soon passing the derelict remains of Kirkstall power-station, and, on the left, the grassy slopes of Gotts Park, at Armley, home of Benjamin Gott, one of the pioneers of Leeds industry.

Look to the right now for the dark outline of Kirkstall Abbey, one of the finest early Cistercian ruins in the country, surrounded by an area of parkland and, amazingly so close to the centre of Leeds, open arable farmland going down to the river. This is one of the amazing features of the Airedale line – the sudden contrast between town and country. Along much of the route the relics of the Industrial Revolution have blended into a rejuvenated nature – birch and willow trees screening dereliction. The road journey between Leeds and Keighley is relatively drab, dominated by between-the-wars ribbon development, but the railway inhabits a remarkably lovely green corridor, in which the old Airedale, truly one of the Yorkshire Dales, makes its presence felt.

The big GKN steelworks beyond the abbey occupies the site of Kirkstall Forge, founded, like much other industry in Yorkshire, by the Cistercian monks, and still flourishing on the same site. But look almost immediately to the left, to the lovely sweep of Calverley Woods, with the canal and woods forming a beautiful rural scene. Soon the Wharfedale line is climbing away to the right, and the train is passing Woodhouse Grove School, until 1965 served by Apperley Bridge Station, one of many quite busy suburban stations axed as a result of the Beeching Report.

A lovely wooded area of valley now, passing the edge of Esholt sewage works on the right which until the 1960s had its own railway line, the steam locomotives being adapted to burn oil from wool waste. One of the locomotives survives as prize exhibit in Bradford Industrial Museum at Moorside Mills. The train plunges into Thackley Tunnel, at 1,496 yards the longest on the line. the tunnel avoids a circuitous route followed by river and canal, which are rejoined for the final mile into Shipley, with the Wharfedale line Bradford link coming in from the right.

There were once two railway stations at Shipley, the second being the old Great Northern line from Laisterdyke and Eccleshill which came down from Thackley by a murderously steep gradient before reaching the little station on the Leeds road, which closed as long ago as 1931 and is now Len's Scooters shop.

The present Shipley Station owes its extraordinary triangular format to the fact that it was originally a junction on the old Leeds–Bradford Railway, taken over by the Midland Railway in the 1840s. After the Beeching closure of 1965 the surviving Leeds–Skipton train had to reverse on to the Bradford–Keighley platforms, a complex and time-wasting procedure that was finally eliminated in 1979 when a new platform–Platform 5 was built–now used by the majority of trains between Leeds and Skipton, in both directions, the southbound service switching tracks just before the curve to reach the platform. The local Bradford–Keighley services use Platform 2 in both directions.

Shipley is a pleasant town with a modern market-place and shopping centre. During the summer months from Wharf Street (about 50 yards below the main Leeds road traffic lights) the Metro water bus, operated by Apollo Canal Carriers of Shipley, operates between Shipley Wharf, Saltaire, and Bingley. Single and return tickets are available making it possible to catch the water bus and return by train from Bingley. For details of the current timetable ring Bradford 595914.

Just ¾ mile from Shipley is Saltaire, a superbly restored little station. Having been closed in 1965 it was, thanks to the efforts of the West Yorkshire Passenger Transport Executive reopened in 1984 with much pomp and circumstance, and justifiably so, the last station to be opened before abolition of the metropolitan county. By any standards Saltaire is a jewel which richly merits exploration. Founded by the great Sir Titus Salt in the 1860s (and named by him–Salt-Aire–with due Victorian modesty), a 'model' mill village away from the slums and pollution which then existed in central Bradford. The magnificent mill straddling the canal with its great Venetian camapanile has long been a show-piece, as has the Victoria Hall (now the Library), the school, the canteen, the almshouses, and the fine open streets all named after the Salt family, and well-designed houses, and a particularly fine Congregational church, acknowledged to be one of the finest small Nonconformist churches in England. Take time to call at the fascinating Victorian boat-houses with a lovingly restored parlour, walk through the park to the unique Shipley Glen Tramway, a century-old cable railway which operates most week-ends and holidays and Wednesdays in the summer, to the old-style Pleasure Grounds, and attractive walks at the top of the glen.

But to return to our journey. Bingley has an attractive Midland Station. It is the terminus of the water-bus service, just behind the station, and anyone with an eye for history should walk the canal towpath to see the Three Rise and Five Rise

The newly opened Saltaire Station blends well with the Baroque Chapel, part of the Model Village *(Photo: Stephen Waring)*

'Staircase' locks on the canal, a highly impressive piece of waterway engineering which you will see featured in the Science Museum, South Kensington. In the summer months you are sure to see a boat in the painfully slow process of 'locking through'. Bingley also has a medieval parish church with some windows designed by the Pre-Raphaelite artist Burne-Jones. Myrtle Park sweeps down to the riverside where included in many riverside and woodland walks is Beckfoot Bridge, an early pack-horse bridge, and Druid's Altar rock, setting for a Chartists' meeting in Benjamin Disraeli's novel *Sybil*.

The next station, only ½ mile along the line, is Crossflatts, which was opened in 1982 and is unique in West Yorkshire in that it was the only one of the PTE's reopened stations that was entirely new rather than a rebuild or resiting of a former station. A long, rather less dramatic portion of Airedale now follows, as the line now sweeps in a broad curve below the green slopes of Thwaites Brow into Keighley.

No one would describe Keighley as a pretty place. But the town is close to some magnificent countryside. It is only a short walk, too, to two notable Keighley attractions. Cliffe Castle is an imposing wool-merchant's mansion now transformed to a splendid art gallery and museum, containing, among other attractions, the last Yorkshire hand-weaver's loom and an impressive geological display of Airedale as well as many natural history attractions (open daily except Mondays). East Riddlesden Hall is a fine Jacobean mansion owned by the National Trust (open April-September);

Keighley Station is also the start of the Keighley & Worth Valley Railway, one of the finest and most imaginatively managed of Britain's steam lines, which deserves a full day to explore. There is a Saturday service all the year round, and a daily service in the main spring and summer holiday times, including the whole of July and August. At other times of the year there is a Sunday service between Oxenhope and Haworth. Worth Rail is a public transport service as much as a fun railway, and you can get through tickets from other destinations in Yorkshire, as well as a useful 10 per cent discount for West Yorkshire Day Rover ticket-holders. Each of the stations on the branch has been lovingly restored, with period advertisements and such bits of nostalgia as milk-churns and leather trunks. There are also beautifully preserved steam locomotives, from such giants as the *City of Wells* to little industrial engines. When the engines are not working, you can see them as static displays in the museum at Oxenhope or at Haworth sheds, and there is a shop at Haworth, and a cafeteria (in a railway carriage) at Oxenhope, as well as a refreshment stand at Keighley. At off-peak times, such as Saturday mornings, your train may be a little diesel railcar, but the line is as attractive as the motive power, with interesting views. Haworth, crowded with shops, cafés, an Information Centre, and the Brontë Museum, is a starting-point for many superb walks over the Brontë Moors. If you want to learn something about the line's surroundings, pick up a copy of Hilary Derby's superbly researched *Worth Valley Rail Trail* from the station bookshop which looks at the railway in its setting and suggests many interesting walks between stations. For details of Worth Valley trains ring Haworth 43629.

The last part of the journey between Keighley and Skipton shows rail as a means of transport at its best, a fast journey covering the 9 miles in some twelve minutes compared with the fifteen-twenty minutes or more it takes by car or thirty-two minutes by bus, though had the three stations at Steeton, Kildwick, and Cononley not been closed it would have taken a little longer, serving communities badly deprived of a transport link. Moves are currently afooot to have Cononley reopened. Scenically, the line is attractive, going mainly through open pastureland, low valley bottom land often flooded in winter, so that the line appears to be crossing lakes after heavy rain. You soon pass the level crossing at Steeton, then Airedale Hospital on the left, before Cross Hills and Kildwick and the line curving north to Cononley, the Airedale Fells now more imposing on each side of the broad valley. In no time at all the train is rattling under the new bypass and into Skipton.

Skipton is a fascinating town with much to see and explore, blending as it does the layout of a medieval town with its broad main street below the castle, and the textile town in which both cotton and wool once were important, and above all a Dales market town which is still a focal point of Dales life. There is a splendid Late Norman and Jacobean castle, in an excellent state of repair (open daily), the medieval parish church with monuments of the great Earls of Cumberland, the excellent Craven Museum in the Town Hall, a street market (daily except Tuesdays and Sundays), and a wide variety of shops, cafés, and pubs. There is also a very attractive canal-side area, including the picturesque Springs branch which runs behind the castle walls. This now a landscaped area, behind the old Corn Mill (museum) and leads to Skipton Woods, which are open to the public every afternoon from 2 p.m. Call in at the fine new Information Centre for local material about this beautiful area. Turn right down the Ginnel (Black Walk) immediately outside the station which leads to the bridge over the canal to the Bus Station for local buses to Grassington, Bolton Abbey, and Malham.

Skipton was once quite an important railway junction, with a busy line through to Colne, Burnley, and Manchester, quite one of the most senseless closures of the immediate post-Beeching era, leaving the East Lancashire line ending as a single-track line at Colne and constantly under threat. Another branch still open for freight as far as Swinden Quarry, ran to Grassington and Threshfield, while yet another victim of the Beeching axe ran to Ilkley via Bolton Abbey. Fortunately, the Yorkshire Dales Railway, an enthsiastic voluntary group, have been able to restore a 2-mile section of line from Embsay Station which is now open on most week-ends with regular steam-trains and a museum shop. As resources permit the line is being extended eastwards in the hope that one day perhaps a regular service will be restored between Skipton and Bolton Abbey. Until that happens visitors to the Yorkshire Dales Railway must depend on the Pennine Bus service from Skipton Bus Station to Embsay. There is a Lead Mining Interpretation Centre at Embsay Station.

For the 1987 visitor, the YDR offers unlimited rides on its trains on the day of issue of the passenger's ticket. There is a fully licensed buffet car on most trains—the trains are all corridor. The locomotives, industrial tank engines, the sort one would have seen in quarries, collieries, steelworks, etc. are all brightly liveried. There is a smart station buffet, and a super book and model railway shop, described as "The best in Preservation". Trains operate every Sunday from Easter to October, with Saturday and Tuesday trains during July and August—plus Bank Holidays. Special services run around Bonfire Night and during December for Santa Claus trains. For details of regular and special services, Dated Wine and Dine trains, and the High Summer Murder Mystery and Suspense Tours, write to Yorkshire Dales Railway, The Station, Embsay, Near Skipton, North Yorkshire. Telephone 0756-4727.

## LEEDS AND BRADFORD—ILKLEY

**by Peter Denbigh**

The Wharfedale line links Leeds and Bradford with Ilkley. Less than half of the line actually lies in the valley of the River Wharfe, the rest being in Airedale. Most passengers visiting Ilkley will start their journey in Leeds, though those travelling from the north-west might well make their connection at Shipley.

The Wharfedale line actually starts some 7 miles to the north-west of Leeds at Apperley Junction, the route being shared with Airedale line trains up to this point. Here the train swings away to the right and almost immediately starts its 1 in 60 climb up to Guiseley. The line crosses the River Aire before entering a cutting and passing through two short tunnels. After the tunnels an embankment is crossed, with pleasant sylvan views to the left of the train. The view is terminated by a short cutting which takes the train into Springs Wood in an attractive small valley. This short stretch of line is certainly one of the most scenic parts of the route.

The valley is left through the short Springs Tunnel after which the line from Bradford and Shipley will be seen to the left of the train. Since February 1983, when the lines from Apperley Junction and from Shipley were singled, the two tracks no longer join together, but run side by side for about a mile before converging just before Guiseley Station. The two parallel tracks were the former up and down lines before the singling took place and the old Esholt Junction was removed. Even the signal-box which controlled the junction has now gone, though the space it occupied can be seen on the right.

Readers with an interest in geology should look out for an excellent example of a fault in the strata exposed in the left-hand side of the cutting, which starts just after the point where the Leeds and Bradford lines come alongside each other. A bed of bluish-grey shale suddenly ends and is replaced by a thick bed of millstone grit.

Just before the short Greenbottom Tunnel the earthworks of the old goods spur to Yeadon can be seen climbing away to the right. This line was just over 1 mile long and was apparently never used by regular passenger trains, though a passenger station was built at the Yeadon terminus. Excursion trains did, however, use the line during local holidays. The route would be ideally suited, with a short extension, to serve the Leeds/Bradford Airport.

After Greenbottom Tunnel an empty train will probably be seen standing on the Bradford line. This train is known locally as 'The Shuttle'. It arrives from Bradford some five minutes before our Leeds train and detrains its Ilkley passengers at Guiseley. It then reverses back down the Bradford line to allow the trains first from and then to Leeds to occupy Guiseley Station. Before the station the two single tracks come together, but then immediately divide again into what is now genuine double track which runs all the way to Ilkley.

Guiseley Station has seen many changes in the last twenty years. Its once busy goods yard (to the left of the train after departure for Ilkley) is sadly no more. The last pick-up goods train ran in 1968, but even into the early 1960s two goods engines could often be seen in the yard. The station itself was once a busy parcel distribution centre for the area. The station buildings have now been demolished, though the land released has made a useful extension to the car park, many commuters preferring to leave their cars here and use the train instead of driving over the congested A65 into Leeds.

Guiseley is fortunate in that its industries are rather diverse, so it has fared better than similar woollen textile towns in West Yorkshire after the slump in the industry in the 1970s. Articles made in Guiseley include babies-prams, bathroom fittings, electric motors and lamps, as well as knitting wools and the more traditional woollen cloth. Its ancient parish church, dedicated to St Oswald, lies about ½ mile to the east of the station along Oxford Road. It was in this church that Patrick Brontë, father of Emily, Anne and Charlotte, was married. A hundred yards from the church, down Well Lane, lies Guiseley Wells; a natural spring round which the village grew. This has continued to flow in all but the driest summers.

Before continuing our journey to Ilkley let us take a trip down the Bradford line. This relatively short stretch of line is a little gem and should not be missed, for it conceals within the 4½ miles to Guiseley Junction, Shipley, no less than four tunnels and three viaducts.

Leaving Guiseley Station the Bradford train will quickly pick up speed down the 1 in 60 gradient and soon reach the former Esholt Junction. After crossing a small valley the train enters Esholt Tunnel. On emerging, there is a short wooded section after which the line crosses a seven-arch viaduct. From this there is an extensive view up Airedale, while below the viaduct on the left lies the village of Esholt, more famous as the Beckingdale of the TV serial *Emmerdale Farm*. After the viaduct the site of the former Esholt Station (closed in 1940) is passed, before another longish cutting brings the train on to a second viaduct. To the right of this there is an attractive view up a small valley to the south-east side of Rombalds Moor. Two short tunnels follow, before the train slows for Baildon Station.

This station has had a chequered history. It was closed in January 1953 because of a fall in patronage due to increasing car usage. However, it was reopened temporarily during the Suez Crisis for the very same car-owners now desperately short of petrol. Luckily the station was never demolished, so thanks to funds provided by Bradford Council, it was reopened on a permanent basis again in January 1973.

After the station the line drops through another short cutting before crossing a third viaduct. This spans the Aire Valley and gives the passenger a good view of the town of Shipley across to the right. The viaduct crosses over the main road, a rather polluted River Aire, and finally the Leeds–Liverpool Canal. After the viaduct the line joins the main Airedale route at Guiseley Junction and the train will stop at Platform 3 or 4 at Shipley Station.

Immediately to the right after leaving Shipley Station for Bradford, and extensive scrap-metal works occupies the former Shipley goods yard. Privately owned diesel shunters now work the sidings, a BR engine picking up the loaded trucks several times a week. A new station is planned at Frizinghall, ¾ mile from Shipley. this will replace a former station closed in May 1965 despite considerable usage, particularly by pupils from the nearby Bradford Boys' Grammar School. At this point the train travels alongside a main road into Bradford, before passing the site of Manningham Station, now used by a stonemason. There is much dereliction to the left of the train on its final approach to Bradford Forster Square Station, while above the banking on the right lies the Valley Parade Football Ground. Here a serious fire in the grandstand brought a tragic end to the club's 1984/85 season.

Only two platforms are now in use at Forster Square Station. Even the signal-box has been dismantled, the signals and cross-overs being worked from the box at Shipley. The station once boasted through services to London St Pancras, Paignton, and Glasgow. Its only surviving non-PTE service is a summer Saturdays train to Morecambe. When the off-peak through service to Ilkley was cut back to Guiseley in September 1985, many thought that this would hasten the end for the former Midland station. However, there is renewed hope with the plans for Frizinghall, and the Ilkley service may also be restored soon. A cross-city minibus service now links the station to Bradford Interchange.

Back now to Guiseley to resume our journey to Ilkley. As the train leaves Guiseley the gradient begins to level out and the train crosses the watershed between Wharfedale and Airedale, entering a short rural section between Guiseley and Menston. Across the fields to the left the rear of what is reputedly the world's largest fish and chip restaurant can be seen – the famous Harry Ramsden's. The large wooded hill to the right of the train is Otley Chevin. Aircraft bound for Leeds/Bradford Airport may be seen apparently heading straight for this hill.

As the line begins to descend into Wharfedale it enters a shallow cutting. Immediately at the start of this cutting, on the left-hand side of the tracks, an interesting short freight line once served the nearby Menston Hospital. This line was actually electrified, and ceased operation in 1951. Unfortunately there is very little left to mark its course. The down gradient now increases as the line passes below the main Bradford–Ilkley road and approaches Menston Station. The buildings at Menston Station remain and are typical of those that once stood at every station on the line.

The gradient from Menston down to Burley is 1 in 68. Passengers who are interested in picking out abandoned trackbeds should sit on the right of the train for there was once a trangular layout here linking the present line with Otley and Arthington Junction on the Leeds–Harrogate line. About ½ mile from Menston Station the south–east link of the triangle left our route at Menston Junction. There is little left to see except a shallow cutting curving away on the right. This line was used up to February 1957 by a through Bradford–Harrogate service. The track remained in place until the closure of the Burley–Otley line, and was used by excursion trains to the north-east coast.

The train soon crosses a short embankment which gives the passenger a fine view down Wharfedale. Even the distant Arthington Viaduct on the Leeds–Harrogate line can be seen. Just before Burley the trackbed of the other line from Arthington comes in on the right. This line was closed in 1965 and ended its life carrying just three passenger trains in each direction per day from Ilkley to Leeds via Otley.

Burley's station buildings have been demolished and unfortunately the signal-box also closed at the end of 1985. This means there is now a very long signal section from Ilkley to Guiseley and problems can arise if a train is running late. Burley Station is situated on the southern edge of the village. As the nearest bus stop is over ½ mile away it is well used by the residents who live on this side of the village. The station is also popular with hikers, for a walk of less than a mile up the road from the station will bring one to Burley Woodhead and a wide selection of paths to follow across Rombalds Moor.

After leaving Burley the train travels at some considerable height along the side of the valley. There is a steep slope up to the left, but down on the right are fine views across the valley. The river with the main road in close attendance can be seen in the valley floor. This main road is often badly congested in peak hours and on fine summer Sundays. Rail passengers meanwhile speed on the almost straight track to the next station at Ben Rhydding. This station was built to serve the Ben Rhydding Hydro Hotel, which in Victorian days was popular with the upper classes seeking cures in local mineral waters. A glance up to left as the train stands in Ben Rhydding Station will give a good view of the Cow and Calf rocks. The line is now 'built up' on its final mile into Ilkley. Nothing remains of the Ilkley engine shed, which lay just before the signal-box controlling Ilkley Station, while on the left-hand side the site of the old goods yard is covered by a supermarket with its attendant car park.

Ilkley has been the terminus of the Wharfedale line since May 1965 when the extension to Skipton via Bolton Abbey was closed. Ilkley Station is scheduled for redevelopment, but at the present time remains more or less intact, though only two of its four platforms are served by trains. The former two through platforms (Nos. 3 and 4) stand devoid of their tracks. An old Midland Railway milepost, fixed to a pillar in the middle of Platform 4, proudly proclaims that the distance to London St Pancras is 211¼ miles. The station has been unmanned since October 1968, part of the former passenger facilities now being a restaurant.

The station is ideally situated in the town and is very convenient for the two main shopping areas of The Grove and Brook Street. Just across the main road at the bottom of Brook Street lies the ancient parish church. Remains of Olicana, a Roman fort, are next to the church, while the River Wharfe is just below. Ilkley lies at one end of a long-distance footpath called the 'Dales Way' which follows the river up to its source and then crosses over into the Lake District.

Back now to the station and across the road it is a relatively short but steep climb up to the edge of the famous Ilkley Moor which features in the well-known song. The moor is criss-crossed by many paths. Take the left-hand one from the paddling-pool, which lies at the top of the steepest part of the climb to the moor, and you will soon find yourself at the attractive Ilkley Tarn. More energetic walkers can continue for another mile up the curious Cow and Calf rocks. The views across the valley from here are well worth the climb. Legend has it that a giant, stepping across the valley, knocked off the smaller Calf rock from the larger Cow. Geologists have a more scientific explanation in terms of ice action during the last glacial period. From the Cow and Calf rocks it is possible to follow a path eastward on the crest of the moor and after about 1½ miles descend via Burley Woodhead to catch a train from Burley Station.

Another pleasant and less strenuous walk from the paddling-pool is to follow the road which bears round to the right, and after about ¼ mile take a path to the right along the edge of the moor. This path should be followed until a small reservoir is reached, after which it is possible to descend back to the town through the attractive Heber's Ghyll, a circular walk or some 2 miles. Keener walkers will find the western part of the moor less crowded but at least as attractive.

# 12

# NORTH BY NORTH-WEST: THE JEWEL IN THE CROWN

## SKIPTON–CARNFORTH

**by Colin Speakman**

Skipton Station is a nicely kept example of Midland Railway architecture. Look for the Midland Gryphon (winged dragon) in the stonework over the main entrance, and some very nice ironwork in the station canopies. It is also a properly staffed station, with a friendly, helpful staff willing to sell you a ticket from anywhere to anywhere. And, another advantage for anyone without decent bus or rail connections, there is also a large free car park in the station forecourt.

One of the many oddities of local government and railway management is that while the majority of trains that come into Skipton are, in fact, part of the regular interval Airedale service sponsored by West Yorkshire Passenger Transport Authority (the body that runs local transport in West Yorkshire now that the County Council has been abolished) and the Leeds–Morecambe line is an Eastern Region sponsored service, Skipton Station is part of the Midland Region and administered from Preston, from where the direct railway line and passenger service was withdrawn in 1970. Although technically there is still a rail link via Clitheroe, there is no regular passenger service on it, so any BR official wanting to go from Preston to Skipton either has to travel via Lancaster or go by car.

So Skipton looks two ways at once–eastwards where most of its passengers travel to Leeds, York, and London, and westwards to Lancaster, Carlisle, and Scotland, through some of the most romantic railway scenery in Britain. There are two services west of Skipton – the Leeds–Lancaster–Morecambe service, sometimes called 'The Western Dales line', and that most celebrated of all survivors, the Leeds–Settle–Carlisle itself. At the time of writing there is basically a two- or three-hour interval between trains on the Western Dales line, some trains calling at all stations, others at only a few.

The Western Dales line has been so overshadowed by its more famous rival that it has not really had a fair Press, in that its existence as a possible re-routing line for Settle and Carlisle trains has allowed the infamous closure notices to be issued at all. More soberly, it is a line which complements the S & C, with a different function, of great interest in its own right: no grand engineering feats perhaps, but serving some fascinating places and offering, for the discerning traveller, some superb views from the carriage window, not of S & C grandeur perhaps, but still some of the finest in northern England. And do not forget that the 'Round Robin' Settle–Carlisle tickets available from Skipton and many stations in West Yorkshire and elsewhere allow for round trips over the Settle line to Carlisle returning via Shap and Lancaster and back over the Western Dales line, so it is perfectly possible to take in both routes on a single day ticket or Settle–Carlisle Rover ticket.

The history of the Western Dales line is chequered. Built quite early by the 'little' North Western Railway Company in the 1840s to connect the industrial West Riding with the new Lancaster–Carlisle Railway, it was taken over by the Midland railway in 1859, who planned to use the Clapham–Ingleton–Tebay branch as their main route to Scotland. Failure to reach agreement between the Midland and the 'big' London & North Western Railway at Ingleton led to the building of the Settle–Carlisle line, albeit in the end reluctantly, by the Midland Railway. So the Ingleton–Tebay line languished as a branch line, finally closing in the 1960s, and is now little more than a green way, with a few surviving bridges, through the Lune Valley, instead of becoming perhaps the Midland's crack main line to the North.

Another piece of nonsense was added in the Beeching era when the direct line to Lancaster from Wennington was closed to enable the removal of Green Ayre Station in Lancaster, forcing most travellers to go the 'long way round' via Carnforth, with insult added to injury when the main-line platforms at Carnforth were subsequently removed, making it impossible for travellers from the West Riding to reach the Lake District without changing at Carnforth and Lancaster. Ironically, a more enlightened railway management now realises the importance of Lancaster as destination and junction station, and most trains now not only call at Carnforth, making connections for Furness and Barrow possible, but travel south along the main line to Lancaster –but the present line remains a monument to irrationality of railway-planners in both the 1860s and the 1960s.

Once away from Skipton, the line soon crosses the valley bottom of the Aire Gap, the remnants of the Colne line soon vanishing underneath the new bypass, the Leeds–Liverpool Canal once again rejoining the railway, the wooded slopes of Flasby Fell to the right. Gargrave is quickly reached. This old coaching village, well served by cafés and pubs, is now on the Pennine Way, and offers an extremely attractive 6-mile walk to the top of Airedale – here known as 'Malhamdale' – where a Pennine bus will bring you back to Skipton or Gargrave.

From Gargrave the railway crosses the lowest watershed of the Pennines, with little more than those gentle hillocks of glacial waste known as 'drumlins'. Students of river developments will see some serpentine meanders of the River Aire here, forming ox-bow lakes as it finds its way through the pass. Almost a mile after Gargrave Station an interesting canal-over-river bridge is visible on the left. The line swings northwards now, past the old station at Bell Busk, once the station for Malham and now a private house, before curving through more drumlins and emerging into Lower Ribblesdale and Hellifield.

Hellifield Station is a grand but melancholy site, a riot of wrought iron (see the Midland Gryphons) and glass with all its splendid waiting-rooms and restaurants boarded up and awaiting a threatened demolition man's hammer. Only Listed Building status has saved it so far. This once-important junction was where Lancashire and Yorkshire trains from Blackburn and Clitheroe met the Midland expresses to Glasgow and lunch could be taken in elegant surroundings. In the old days here were engine sheds, locomotives, railwaymen, island platforms, and a railway village which still stubbornly survives the virtual extinction of its once major industry. Freight trains still use the 'Lanky' line, as do the numerous main-line diversions via S & C, together with the monthly Dales Rail service in summer from Preston, which actually calls at Clitheroe Station.

There follows another 1½ miles of Ribblesdale to Long Preson, a village of great charm, despite the non-stop thunderous traffic along the A65 which dominates its centre. The line now turns north-westwards in earnest, along the shallow Ribble Basin before reaching Settle Junction where the Settle–Carlisle begins its spectacular 'Long Drag' northwards and the Western Dales line winds its way across the Ribble.

Giggleswick with its delightful Saxon name, is about a mile from the station and is really the twin village of Settle just across the river, containing the ancient parish church. Settle is only just a little farther away and the station serves both communities. Giggleswick is also the starting-point of a wide choice of walks into Upper Ribblesdale and the Three Peaks area, a favourite being to follow the paths over the limestone crags, that here begin to dominate the scenery to Feizor, Austwick, Crummackdale, and Clapham.

Now follows a beautiful stretch of line through undulating country with magnificent views, to the right, to the limestone uplands of the Yorkshire Dales National Park, and, to the left, over to the gritstone moors that form the Bowland Fells. This is beautiful, lonely, little-known country, only crossed by quiet lanes. Soon the line picks up the little Wenning Valley, a tributary of the Lune, swinging north to Clapham Station.

The contrast with its London namesake could not be greater. Clapham Station is superbly situated at a junction of quiet lanes, the huge expanse of Burn Moor to the left and the dramatic outline of Ingleborough Mountain to the right. This is perfect cycling country, and there is nowhere better to take a bike to get into remote and lovely countryside at the edge of the Forest of Bowland Area of Outstanding Natural Beauty, retuning from Giggleswick, Bentham, or Wennington stations. The village, a full 1¼ miles from the station (though the station is served by a welcoming pub), is extremely attractive, surrounding a delightful wooded stream, with spectacular walks through Clapdale Gorge to Ingleborough Cave, Trow Gill, Gaping Gill, and Ingleborough summit. There is also a National Park Information Centre and a choice of cafés and pubs. Clapham was the birthplace of the great botanist and plant-collector Reginald Farrer (1880–1940), and is also the home of the Dalesman publishing company. The abandoned 'Little NW' route via Ingleton can be seen off to the right immediately after the station.

The Western Dales line continues almost due west now, leaving the central peaks of the Dales for the gentler Wenning and Lune valleys. Bentham, the last station in Yorkshire, is soon reached; Bentham is really two villages, High and Low Bentham, the station serving the former. Both are former industrial villages, the silk industry once being important. Like Clapham, Bentham provides excellent access to the Forest of Bowland, an area far less well known than the Dales, but offering some magnificent opportunities to the serious rambler.

Wennington is a former junction where trains once divided, the main portion of the train continuing down the Lune to Lancaster, a tank engine taking a couple of coaches forward to Carnforth. The former branch is now the main line, and swings north, now through delightful rolling countryside of quite different character to the Dales. Once through the Melling Tunnel, the line swings across the Lune, soon picking up the little River Keel before crossing under the M6 motorway and over the gantries of the high-speed West Coast main line for Carnforth.

Carnforth is a pleasant, typical North Lancashire town, with an impressive station once the setting of the Noël Coward film *Brief Encounter*. There is also Steam Town Rail Museum and workshop with a short walk away, cafés, pubs, and a quite excellent second-hand bookshop. The train now joins the electrified main line for the short run to Lancaster, with views of Morecambe Bay on the right *en route*. But let us return now to that railway junction below Settle, where the Settle–Carlisle line leaves for the Long Drag.

# THE SETTLE–CARLISLE LINE

**by Colin Speakman**

The dramatic success of the new Dalesman stopping service along the Settle–Carlisle line has repercussions which are too complex to be fully explored here, but in brief terms the new daily train service offers opportunity to explore this magnificent railway and its surrounding countryside in a way which hitherto was only possible on some twelve or so days a year when Dales rail charter train services operated. Suddenly every day is a Dales Rail day, a superb new service and leisure opportunity which promises to open up the Yorkshire Dales and the Eden Valley to many more visitors. Although only three stations – Settle, Horton, and Ribblehead are actually in Yorkshire, two more–Dent and Garsdale–are within the Yorkshire Dales National Park, and are 'Yorkshire' in all but a narrow bureaucratic sense, having been transferred to Cumbria in 1974.

There is so much to do and see from the Settle–Carlisle that the pity of it is that there is only space to outline highlights – like Settle itself, a beautifully preserved Midland station in an elevated position giving splendid views across the Ribble to Giggleswick and the Bowland Fells. Go to Settle on market day (Tuesdays) and enjoy the bustle and colour of its little crowded square. Climb up Castlebergh Rock or get up to Victoria Cave (the Tourist Office in the Town Hall will give directions).

Immediately beyond Settle the ascent of the Long Drag begins in earnest, and so does the spectacular engineering, with river, road, and railway fighting for space in the narrow river gorge – Langcliffe Scar is the notable crag soon passed on the right, and Taitlands Tunnel was built to hide the smoky railway from the sight of a local landowner. The line follows a deep cutting below Stainforth with its Youth Hostel, waterfall, and famous pack-horse bridge, emerging by Helwith Bridge and its unsightly quarries, now no longer served by the rail line that helped to create them. To the right, however, are the first of several spectacular views of the Sphinx-like Pen-y-Ghent at 2,277 feet high the lowest of the Three Peaks but an impressive summit by anyone's standards. Horton in Ribblesdale, the first of the eight stations brought back into regular service on 14 July 1986 is the perfect starting-point for a climb of Pen-y-Ghent or Ingleborough, a climb of which can be combined with a walk to Ribblehead. Horton also has the excellent Pen-y-Ghent Café and Stores, a café which specialises in the needs of hill-walkers and outdoor people.

From Horton you are in epic countryside, a wild, increasingly lonely landscape shared only by a few sheep and a few curlews, as you climb in the train a countryside dominated by the bare, sculptured shapes of the great land masses, a gigantic landscape, relieved only by the odd line of characteristic 'Derby gothic' style railway cottages.

Then Ribblehead Station, sadly with only a single surviving platform, which is situated in the vast bowl of empty Three Peaks landscape, nevertheless a good place to finish a walk and return from, with the welcoming Station Inn, open in good time before the last train down the valley. Interestingly enough, Ribblehead now has one of the most curious commuter trains in Britain – 07.22 departure for Leeds for an entire population in the hamlet of about six!

From Ribblehead the track singles and makes its somewhat nervous way across the great twenty-four-arch viaduct, by common consent now suffering the effects of old age and neglect in the dreadful Pennine climate, as storms and gales roar their way through the gap between the massive bulk of Ingleborough to the left and Whernside ahead.

Now the train roars into Blea Moor Tunnel, well over a mile of inky blackness, to emerge, with gloriously dramatic effect, on a moorland shelf high above Dentdale,

*Black Five* hauls the West Yorkshire 'Dalesman' through the forbidding Pennine landscape in March 1986, as a curtain-raiser to the TUCC hearings *(Photo: Denis Thorpe, reproduced courtesy of The Guardian)*

over Dentdale and Artengill viaducts, 1,100 feet above sea-level and so high that people in the valley below cannot believe their eyes as they see a train crossing the side of the high fell. This must surely be the finest view from any railway-carriage window in England. There is Dent Station, at 1,150 feet the highest main-line station in Britain, and a marvellous place to start a day's walk, down into the 'green paradise' of Dentdale to Dent, a welcoming village the best part of 4 miles from the station serving it. Look at the old snow fences on the hillside and reflect how, in hard winters in days gone by, whole engines vanished into the cuttings here, only their funnels peering pathetically above the drifts. Through Rise Hill Tunnel the train now climbs above the shoulder of Garsdale, pulling into Garsdale Station.

Garsdale Station is a popular station for visitors and local people from Hawes and Sedbergh, being an excellent starting-point for a wide choice of walks at the top end of both Garsdale and Wensleydale. Once the station was known as 'Hawes Junction', the terminating-point of trains from Northallerton and Leyburn with an engine shed, turntable, and water-tanks filling the highest set of steam-engine water-troughs in the British Isles. At least there is now a minibus service to Hawes and Sedbergh (telephone 0756 752748 for information of its period of operation) and, with the new Dalesman service, Garsdale Head, with its long row of railwaymen's cottages, is once again a place of some significance.

From Garsdale the line curves north across the lovely Dandry Mire Viaduct to the top end of Wensleydale and Hell Gill for the final ascent to Aisgill summit, 1,169 feet above sea-level, the source of the River Eden and the watershed of all England. Here we finally take our leave of Yorkshire. Within a short distance the line has followed rivers flowing south (Ribblesdale), west (Dentdale and Garsdale), east (Wensleydale), and now north in the Eden Valley.

In Cumbria now (or Westmorland for the traditionalists), Mallerstang is the name given to the valley formed by the Upper Eden, one of the very few rivers of any importance in England that flows northwards. It is a grandly impressive gorge, bounded on one side by the craggy line of Mallerstang Edge rising to High Seat, above Swaledale, and on the other side to the impressive bulk of Wild Boar Fell, a magnificent peak which provides some of the finest fell-walking in all England with views, in clear weather, which extend to the Scottish hills beyond the Solway. You pass, on the right, the ruins of Pendragon Castle, a Late Norman castle whose name indicates Celtic origins (Uther Pendragon was reputedly the name of King Arthur's father) and, just visible on the skyline to the right, a hill with nine cairns, Nine Standards Rigg where, according to legend, standards or flags were raised by local Dalesmen to make a marauding Scots army believe that attack was imminent.

Kirkby Stephen lies at the edge of a complex area of geological change, marked by the great Pennine fault which crosses the line near Birkett Tunnel, making this a difficult section of line to build, over difficult, high land, before entering the rich Permain Red Sandstone country of the Eden Valley. Kirkby Stephen Station lies 1½ miles from the town it serves. There once were two stations – the other, Kirkby Stephen East lay closer to the town on the old Tebay–Barnard Castle line over Stainmore and has been closed for many years. Kirkby Stephen Station has been refurbished thanks to enthusiastic voluntary help, with new notice-boards and signs, flower-beds and flower-pots, and a reopened waiting-room on the 'up' platform. There is also a minibus service which operates to Kirkby Stephen town and Brough, thus eliminating a dreary and dangerous walk on the A685. The town has great charm, with interesting church and market-place, and pleasant riverside walks, shops, and a choice of pubs and cafés.

The line now crosses the mouth of the great Stainmore Pass, one of the most important crossings of the Pennines since Roman times, and now traversed by the busy A66 trunk road between the A1 and the M6. You soon cross Smardale Viaduct – look to the left to see the other Smardale Viaduct on the Stainmore line, in a lovely wooded valley. This viaduct recently only narrowly escaped demolition, and it is hoped will be preserved as a monument.

You are now in Border Country, and you will notice not only the familiar Red Sandstone and even architectural styles reminiscent of Dumfriesshire, but, in villages like Crosby Garret, to the right just beyond Smardale, notice the fortified farmhouse, so built to defend the inhabitants in late medieval times against the raids of marauding Scots. The Scots now travel past in more friendly style along the Settle–Carlisle line.

There is pleasant but less dramatic country now across the Eden Valley, but look ahead, right, towards the massive bulk of the North Pennines, which increasingly dominate the Settle–Carlisle line's northern sections. A surviving remnant of the Stainmore line, the Warcop Ministry of Defence branch, serves the great firing-ranges which now dominate this corner of the North Pennines.

Soon Appleby is in sight, the compact little town astride the River Eden, until 1974 the county town of Westmorland, worth a few hours of anyone's time – its jewel of a market square, fine old church, where Lady Anne Clifford and her mother lie buried, almshouses, little pubs and shops, woodland and riverside walks, and a magnificent Norman castle set in impressive grounds, open to visitors during the summer months.

Appleby is a good place to end a Yorkshire trip along the S & C. Those continuing by the equally attractive but less spectacular line to Carlisle should refer to our companion volume, *Lancashire and Cumbria by Rail*, for a description of this section. But before you leave, note the slate plaque on the station wall, a memorial to the late Bishop of Wakefield, the Reverend Eric Treacy who died on 13 May 1978 while photographing *Evening Star*, Britain's last steam giant, as it approached Appleby Station. 'The Railway Bishop' was fond of referring to Hadrian's Wall, York Minster, and the Settle & Carlisle Railway as the three great man-made wonders of the North of England. He loved the S & C and recorded its heroic last days of steam in photographs of poetic splendour. He could not have had a more fitting memorial.

# POSTSCRIPT–A NOTE ON CLOSURES

This is the section we would rather not have had to write. But there is no avoiding the fact that Yorkshire has recently had more than its fair share of lines up for closure. When this book was being assembled in 1986 there were in fact five closure proposals pending. These were:

1. The Cudworth line–the ex-Midland route between Normanton and Rotherham.
2. The 'Five Curves'–the Huddersfield–Halifax line and some related curves.
3. Huddersfield–Denby Dale–Penistone.
4. Leeds–Castleford/Normanton via Woodlesford.
5. Settle–Carlisle.

A sixth line, Goole–Gilberdyke, was also proposed, but following agreement with Humberside County Council to finance repairs to the bridge at Goole (made necessary by the seemingly incurable tendnency of shipping to collide with it), this line has been reprieved–for the time being at least.

By the end of 1986 all the TUCC hearings into these closures (presided over in charactistic style by James Towler) had been completed. These started with a modest half-day session on the Cudworth line in Wakefield in June 1984, climaxed with the record-breaking sixteen-day mobile marathon on the Settle & Carlisle in April 1986, and concluded with a two-day hearing on Woodlesford in October 1986 to coincide with bus deregulation!

On 3 December the first decisions were announced by the Transport Secretary, John Moore, unconditionally approving the Cudworth and 'Five Curves' closures. Meantime however, a number of other changes were taking place. Firstly, much to everyone's surprise the effect of bus deregulation (initially at any rate) was to the benefit of rail, as passengers voted with their feet against the confusion and uncertainty of deregulation. Secondly in West Yorkshire, the extension of the County 'Metrocard' ticket to rail, had produced an upsurge in rail patronage. These factors (together with some changes to the accounting system governing PTE rail support) placed the new Passenger Transport Authority in the happy position of being able to announce that they would support both the Denby Dale and Woodlesford services, thereby effectively lifting the threat to these lines for the time being.

The outcome of the Settle–Carlisle case looks like being rather longer in coming, as the Government (mindful perhaps of electoral considerations) have now accepted the need for further studies into the financial and engineering aspects. If this line too is saved, it will, like the other two, be principally because (for whatever reason) *more people are using it.* This lesson cannot be too strongly emphasised, as the present moderately encouraging climate could as easily be reversed, placing almost any secondary line in Yorkshire at risk once again. (And there is always the lingering threat posed to the bridges at Goole and Selby by rogue shipping!) So, as many a local users' group have found, *use it or lose it!* And that applies equally to visitors as to local residents.

Barely was the last TUCC report off the presses than a sour note was introduced in March 1987 by the peremptory and somewhat undignified dismissal of Mr James Towler from his post as Chairman of the North East (previously Yorkshire) Transport Users' Consultative Committee. Many Yorkshire members of the Railway Development Society will testify to the sympathetic hearing and support they have received in the many proceedings he has presided over. It is fervently to be hoped that his successor will continue in the same tradition.

# COME AND JOIN US!

The Railway Development Society is a national, voluntary, independent body which campaigns for better services, for both passengers and freight, and greater use of rail transport.

It publishes books and papers, holds meetings, stages exhibitions, sometimes runs special trains, and generally endeavours to put the case for rail to politicians, civil servants, commerce and industry, and the public at large; as well as feeding users' comments and suggestions to British Rail management and unions.

Membership is open to all who are in general agreement with the aims of the Society, and subscriptions (June 1987) are:

Standard rate:£7.50

Reduced rate: (for pensioners, full-time students) £4.00

Families: £7.50 (plus £1 for each member of the household)

Write to the National Membership Secretary, Mr F.J. Hastilow, 21 Norfolk Road, Sutton Coldfield, West Midlands, B75 6SQ.

For details of *Yorkshire branch* activities write to the Branch Secretary, Dennis Bradbury, 59 Dore Road, Sheffield, S17 3ND.

There are many Line Users' Groups in Yorkshire, most of whom are affiliated to the RDS. The full list is as follows:

*Friends of the Settle–Carlisle Line Association*
Secretary: Peter Shaw, 33 Temple Ridding Drive, Baildon, BD17 5PX.

*Goole and District Rail Action Group*
Secretary: John Dargan, 23 Grosvenor Avenue, Goole, DN14 6UT.

*Halifax and District Rail Action Group*
Secretary: Steve Waring, 65 Springwood Avenue, Halifax, HX3 0UT.

*Halifax–Huddersfield Rail Travellers' Association*
Secretary: R.J. Corner, Scoutfield, Scout Road, Mytholmroyd, Halifax.

*Huddersfield–Penistone–Sheffield Rail Users' Association*
Secretary: Andrew Oldfield, 14 Long Lane, Worrall, Sheffield, S30 3AF.

*Knaresborough–Harrogate Rail Users' Association*
Secretary: Jim Rogers, 17 Grove Street, Starbeck, Harrogate, HG2 7PH.

*Missing Link (Spen Valley Line)*
Secretary: Nigel Cross, 1 Anroyd Street, Dewsbury, WF13 4LT.

*Pontefract and District Rail Action Group*
Secretary: David Pickersgill, 171 Lower Oxford Street, Castleford, WF10 4AQ.

*Sheffield Passengers' Association*
Secretary: Dr Hugh Porteous, 115 Wollaton Road, Sheffield, S17 4LF.

*Todmorden Rail Action Group*
Secretary: Michael Steed, Wood Cottage, Ewood Lane, Todmorden, OL14 7DF.

*Upper Calder Valley Transport Action Group*
Secretary: D.C. Kershaw, 2 Beaumont Street, Todmorden, OL14 5JZ.

*Wharfedale Rail Users' Group*
Secretary: Derek Joanes, 13 Brooklands Lane, Menston, Ilkley, LS29 6PL.

Mention should be made of :

*Friends of Dales Rail*
Secretary: Mrs S. Barass, 3 Rochester Terrace, Leeds, LS6 3DF

*Transport 2000 (West Yorkshire Group)*
Secretary: Alan Haigh, 2 Foster Close, Morley, Leeds, LS27 9NH.

# FURTHER INFORMATION

**Tourist Information**

*Yorkshire and Humberside Tourist Board*
312 Tadcaster Road, York, YO2 2HF. Telephone 0904 707961

Local Tourist Information can be obtained from the following offices:

| | |
|---|---|
| *Barnsley* 56 Eldon St | 0226 206757 |
| *Bradford* Hall Ings | 0274 753678 |
| *Bridlington* Prince Street | 0262 673474 |
| *Doncaster* Waterdale | 0302 734309 |
| *Goole* Carlisle Street | 0405 2187 |
| *Halifax* Piece Hall | 0422 68725 |
| *Harrogate* Crescent Road | 0423 525666 |
| *Huddersfield* Albion Street | 0484 22133 |
| *Hull* Albion Street | 0482 223344 |
| *Leeds* Wellington Street | 0532 462454 |
| *Rotherham* Walker Place | 0707 382121 |
| *Scarborough* St Nicholas Cliff | 0723 373333 |
| *Selby* Park Street Bus Station | 0757 703263 |
| *Sheffield* Union Street | 0742 734671 |
| *Skipton* Victoria Square | 0756 2809 |
| *Wakefield* Wood Street | 0924 370211 |
| *York* Exhibition Square | 0904 21756 |
| *York* The Railway Station | 0904 643700 |

**Transport Information**

*British Rail:* Principal Telephone Enquiry Offices in Yorkshire are:

| | | |
|---|---|---|
| *Doncaster* 0302 20191–4 | *Hull* 0482 26033 | *Leeds* 0532 448133 |
| *Scarborough* 0723 373486 | *Sheffield* 0742 726411 | *York* 0904 642155 |

*Bus Information* can best be obtained from County/PTE Offices as follows:

The Public Transport Co-ordinator, Humberside County Council
Manor Road, Beverley, HU17 7BX 0482 867131

The Public Transport Co-ordinator, North Yorkshire County Council
County Hall, Northallerton, DL7 8AH 0609 3123

South Yorkshire Passenger Transport Executive
Exchange Street, Sheffield, S2 5SZ 0742 768688

West Yorkshire Passenger Transport Executive
Metro House, West Parade, Wakefield, WF1 1NS 0924 378234

Bus Station enquiry offices in the principal towns are as follows:

Barnsley 0226 202555
Bradford 0274 732237
Bridlington 0262 673142
Doncaster 0302 60121
Halifax 0422 64467
Harrogate 0423 66061
Huddersfield 0484 545444
Hull – City 0482 2222
Hull – Country 0482 27142
Leeds 0532 457676
Rotherham 0707 563563
Scarborough 0723 375463
Selby 0757 703263
Sheffield 0742 755655
Skipton 0756 5331
Wakefield 0924 375555
York 0904 24161

One other important address – the passengers' guardian angel:
*Transport Users' Consultative Committee for North-east England*
Hilary House, 16 St Saviours Place, York, YO1 2PL 0904 25615

**Map Information**

Yorkshire is a big place, so you will need a lot of maps to cover the whole of it. For example, no less than eleven sheets of the Ordnance Survey 1:50 000 Landranger Series are needed to cover all the lines described in this book, but four of them (Sheets 104, 105, 110, 111) effectively cover Metropolitan Yorkshire, and Sheet 98 the southern half of the Settle–Carlisle line. Those who do not intend venturing far from the train will find a smaller scale map adequate, such as the Batholomew 1:100 000 National Series (Sheets 29, 32, 33, 35, 36) or the OS 1:250000 Routemaster Sheets 5 or 6,– both these sheets cover most but not all Yorkshire – irritatingly Sheet 5 excludes the part east of a line through Market Weighton and Sheet 6 excludes the part west of a line through Malham! For the walker or cyclist requiring a larger scale, particular mention should be made of the OS 1:25 000 Outdoor Leisure Maps which cover some of the best upland areas of Yorkshire including Sheet 1 (The Peak District), Sheet 21 (South Pennines), Sheet 10 (Malham and Upper Wharfedale), Sheet 2 (The Three Peaks), and Sheets 26 and 27 (North York Moors). Other areas are covered by the (even more numerous) Pathfinder series at the same scale. All these are available from any good bookshop in all major towns. A number of other useful maps are produced by the Yorkshire and Humberside Tourist Board, and can be obtained from the various tourist offices at the addresses listed.

**West Yorkshire County Cycle Route**

One of the last acts of the County Council before abolition was to create a signposted 150-mile Cycle Route round the scenic fringes of the county, mostly on minor roads, and passing a dozen local rail stations *en route*. A free leaflet giving details is available from Tourist Information Offices in West Yorkshire or direct from The Joint Countryside Unit, Chantry House, 123 Kirkgate, Wakefield, WF1 1YG (telephone 0924 367111 Extension 4701/4761), or from the various District Council Countryside Services.

**Other Books in this Series**

*East Anglia by Rail*
*Midlands by Rail*
*Five Shires by Rail*
*North East by Rail*
*Kent and East Sussex by Rail*
*Cheshire and North Wales by Rail*
*Lancashire and Cumbria by Rail*
*South West by Rail*
*Scotland by Rail*

All the above are obtainable from the RDS Sales Officer, Mr Geoff Kent, 21 Fleetwind Drive, East Hunsbury, Northampton, NN4 0ST, from the respective local branches, from bookshops, or from the publishers, Jarrold Colour Publications, Barrack St., Norwich NR3 1TR.

**Acknowledgements**

Apart from our authors and photographers, thanks are due to firstly, Mr C.F.D. Cooper of Bracknell, Berks but previously of Sheffield, who kindly donated a sum of money towards the expense of producing this book: secondly, Dr and Mrs Hugh Porteous who undertook the task of word-processing, thereby greatly easing the task of the editors; and thirdly, Mr and Mrs Hyomes who played host to the 'editorial committee' on two occasions.

# SELECT BIBLIOGRAPHY


**Railways**

K.Hoole, *A Regional History of the Railways of Great Britain*, Volume 4 – *NorthEast England* (David & Charles).

D.Joy, *A Regional History of the Railways of Great Britain*, Volume 8 – *South and West Yorkshire* (David & Charles).

A.Haigh and D.Joy, *Yorkshire Railways* (Dalesman Books).

D.Joy, *Railways in the North*, (Dalesman Books).

K.Hoole, *Railways of the Yorkshire Dales*, (Dalesman Books).

J.Bushell, *The World's Oldest Railway,* (Turntable Publications).

J.Bushell, *Yorkshire's First Main Line,* (West Yorks Transport Museum).

S.Batty, *Rail Centres: Sheffield,* (Ian Allan).

K.Hoole, *Rail Centres: York,* (Ian Allan).

J.S.Whiteley and G.W.Morrison, *British Railways Past and Present – No. 2 South & West Yorkshire,* (Silver Link Publications, Carnforth).

J.Farline and P.Cookson, *Railways Around Wakefield and Pontefract,* (Wyvern Publications)

M.Bairstow, *Railways Around Harrogate,* (Wyvern Publications).

M.Bairstow, *The Sheffield, Ashton-under-Lyne and Manchester Railway,* (M.Bairstow).

S.Bain, *Railroaded! Battle for Woodhead Pass,* (Faber & Faber).

M.Bairstow, *The Huddersfield & Sheffield Junction Railway,* (M.Bairstow).

M.Bairstow, *The Leeds, Huddersfield & Manchester Railway,* (M.Bairstow).

M.Bairstow, *The Great Northern Railway in West Yorkshire,* (Wyvern Publications).

M.Bairstow, *Railways Through Airedale and Wharfedale,* (Wyvern Publications).

D.Binns, *The Scenic Settle & Carlisle Railway,* (Wyvern Publications).

W.R.Mitchell and D.Joy, *Settle to Carlisle,* (Dalesman Books).

S.Abbott, *To Kill a Railway,* (Leading Edge Press & Publishing).

**Public Transport**

A.E.Jones, *Roads and Rails of West Yorkshire 1890 – 1950,* (Ian Allan).

C.Speakman, *Public Transport in West Yorkshire – 10 Years of Achievement,* (West Yorkshire PTE).

**General Interest**

C.Speakman, *Wayfarer Walks in the South Pennines,* (Dalesman Books).

M.Pocock, *York,* (Dalesman Books).

J.Curd, *Scarborough,* (Dalesman Books).

J.Curd, *The Yorkshire Coast,* (Dalesman Books).

K.Parry, *Trans-Pennine Heritage – Hills People and Transport,* (David & Charles).

J.Ogden, *Yorkshire's River Aire,* (T.Dalton).

J.Ogden, *Yorkshire's River of Industry,* (T.Dalton).

J.Ogden, *Yorkshire's River Derwent,* (T.Dalton).

Nikolaus Pevsner, *The Buildings of England.* Three volumes to cover Yorkshire – East, North and West Ridings, (Penguin Books).



Acknowledgements for assistance in the compilation of this list to:
*The Transport Scene* 35 Westgate End, Wakefield (telephone 0924 – 363715) – five minutes' walk from Wakefield Westgate Station (away from the town).
"Possibly the largest stock of transport books in the North of England". Also second-hand book section and a mail-order service.
Also useful: *Austicks* Bookshops. 64 The Headrow, Leeds, produce a free booklist of titles on Yorkshire.

# INDEX



Beverley Minster, a big church for a small town (*Photo: Steve Oakley*)

ISBN 0–7117–0296–9



Published and printed in Great Britain by Jarrold and Sons Ltd, Norwich. 187.